HOW TO COMMUNICATE

THE RIGHT WAY

3 Manuscripts in 1 Book, Including: How to Talk to People, How to Ask Questions and How to Be Funny

Dean Mack

More by Dean Mack

Discover all books from the Social Skills Best Seller Series by Dean Mack at:

bit.ly/dean-mack

Book 1: *How to Flirt*

Book 2: *How to Start a Conversation*

Book 3: *How to Talk to People*

Book 4: *How to Ask Questions*

Book 5: *How to Be Funny*

Book 6: *How to Influence People*

Book 7: *How to Attract Men*

Book 8: *How to Attract Women*

Themed book bundles available at discounted prices:

bit.ly/dean-mack

Table of Contents

HOW TO
TALK TO PEOPLE
THE RIGHT WAY
The Only 7 Steps You Need to Master
Conversation Skills, Effective Communication
and Conversation Tactics Today
DEAN MACK

BOOK 1: HOW TO TALK TO PEOPLE

THE RIGHT WAY

The Only 7 Steps You Need to Master Conversation Skills, Effective Communication and Conversation Tactics Today

Dean Mack

Table of Contents

Introduction

Learning how to talk effectively is important. Whether you want it or not, there is a constant flow of communication that happens everywhere. In fact, even if you choose not to talk, you still communicate a message to those around you. In the world today, communication remains as important as it has always been thousands of years ago. After all, before robots and computers can do their job, there must first be human interaction — and the best way to interact with another human being is by using effective communication techniques.

The following chapters will teach you everything that you need to know about mastering the art of talking to people and communicating effectively.

Chapter 1 lays down the basics, so that you will have a strong foundation and understanding of what effective communication is all about.

Chapter 2 reveals the 7 steps that you need to master the art of talking to people. This part of the book reveals what you need to learn to become a highly-effective communicator.

Chapter 3 discusses the best practices of effective communication. Learn additional tips and tricks that can further develop your communication skills.

May this book be your guiding light to success and a happier life.

Chapter 1: The Basics

What is effective communication?

Being able to communicate is a vital element of humanity. The history of communication can be traced back to the time when warriors would form a circle around a bonfire and exchange stories with one another. Today, there are so many ways and means to communicate: You can send a text message, write an email, make a phone call, and others. Still, nothing beats face-to-face communication as being the most personal and effective manner of talking with another human being.

There are many definitions of what communication is. According to Merriam Webster's Dictionary, communication is "the act or process of using words, sounds, signs, or behaviors to express or exchange information or to express your ideas, thoughts, feelings, etc., to someone else." Simply put, communication is about expressing yourself to another person. It is worth noting that many people know how to communicate — even a baby communicates with her parents. However, only a few know how to communicate effectively, in a way that people will really hear and understand what you are trying to express. This book is about *effective* communication, which is about being able to communicate your thoughts, feelings, and ideas, clearly and more effectively. This is about having a real conversation with another human being.

Is it important to learn effective communication? This is a legitimate question. After all, most people do not know how to communicate effectively and merely say whatever ideas they may have in mind, so why would anyone bother to learn effective communication? Of course, you are free to decide whether or not you want to take the effort to learn how to talk effectively. You can stay the way that you are right now, but you can also improve your communication skills and see the significant and positive difference that it can do to your life.

People who know how to communicate effectively tend to be more successful in life. They are also the ones who establish a good network of connections. This is because human beings like people who communicate clearly and effectively. Take note that this is not just about having a conversation, but effective communication also means making the other person feel good about having a conversation with you. As you can see, true effective communication is not just about expressing your thoughts and ideas to another. It goes beyond the simple definition of what communication is all about and also takes into consideration the whole communication process, as well as the entire experience of having a conversation.

Have you noticed people who seem to be able to command a whole audience just by talking? How about people who are able to carry on a conversation for hours yet still capture the attention and interest of his audience? These people are the ones who communicate effectively. Of course, effective communication does not just work before a crowd of people. It also works powerfully in a one-on-one conversation setup. These days, many people have the habit of communicating; however, they do not do so effectively. In fact, many people are poor communicators and barely manage to get a message across clearly. If you learn and practice the techniques in this book that will turn you into a real effective communicator, then you can set yourself apart and have your own brand. People will like talking with you. In fact, they will like you as a person. This, of course, can open lots of doors of opportunity. Learning to communicate effectively can change your life, as well as the life of the people you talk to. It simply has its own magic that can create a positive impact.

The communication process

The communication process refers to a process whereby two or more people exchange information. Take note that it is an *exchange* of information and not just about sending information to another. Hence, it is a two-way process where the parties take turns to talk and listen to each other.

The communication process has 6 parts or elements. Let us take a look at them one by one:

➢ Sender

The sender is the one that starts the communication process. The sender is also referred to as the *source*. The sender has an information, thought, or idea, or even an emotion that he would like to share to another. In order to do this, he will have to encode the message in a form that will be understood by another, and then transmit the message.

➢ Receiver

Once the message of a sender is transmitted, it is directed to a receiver, or the person to whom the sender is talking to and to whom he wishes to convey the said information. Once the receiver receives the message coming from the sender, he will then have to decode it. This is the reason why the language used by the sender should be something that the receiver understands so that he (the receiver) will easily be able to decode the message and understand what the sender is trying to express.

➢ Message

Obviously, this refers to the information that the sender wants to communicate to the receiver. If you combine the sender, receiver, and the message, altogether, then you have the most basic elements of a communication process. However, the process does not really end there.

➢ Medium

The medium is also referred to as the *channel*. It simply refers to the means that the sender uses to send his message. For example, a text message can be sent using a mobile phone as the medium.

➢ Feedback

At the basic level a communication is complete once the sender is able to transmit his message and the said message is receiver by the receiver. However, it is not the end of the process. Once the receiver has received the message, he then responds to the sender. This is to indicate that he has received and understood the message. A feedback usually keeps the communication process active and on-going. It can be verbally made or even in writing. It can even be expressed through one's actions.

➢ Other factors

The communication process is also subject to other elements that may affect how the information is sent, received, and understood:

Noise - A noise usually comes in the form of interference that makes the information difficult to be understood. It can refer to the actual noise in the environment which makes it hard for the receiver to even hear the voice of the sender, or it can also refer to the static interference when communication over the phone.

Anything that hinders the communication process may be considered a noise.

Context - The context by which something is transmitted can affect how the other person would understand it. This, of course, can affect the quality of the exchange of information. This may have some social and cultural aspect into it. Hence, before you transmit any message, be sure to do so in the right context in order to avoid misunderstanding. For example, to the Chinese, calling them as *intsik*, which is just another term for *Chinese*, is considered insulting. Hence, when you are talking with a Chinese person, do not include the word *intsik* when you transmit a message; otherwise, the receiver might feel insulted even if you are saying something pleasant.

Time element - Time can also be considered another factor. This refers to the time when the receiver gets to receive or read the message transmitted by the sender. This normally applies in cases where you are not engaged in a face-to-face conversation. For example, when you communicate via email or text messaging. You cannot always be sure that the receiver will be able to get your message immediately after you send it.

It is worth noting that effective communication means so much more than knowing the communication process. Being aware of this process is only good in order to help you understand how a communication normally takes place, but being a truly effective communicator means so much more than knowing how the process works. This, however, can give you a good idea on how you can communicate more effectively.

Is it for you?

Many people are aware of the term *effective communication*, but only a few are truly able to communicate effectively. So, is it for you? The good news is that effective communication is for everyone. This is because anyone can learn it. However, just like anything that is worth learning, you will need to dedicate your time and efforts to it. This is not something that you can just learn overnight. It takes practice and commitment to become an effective communicator, but it is nevertheless learnable and doable.

The following chapters will walk you through the 7 steps that will turn you into an effective communicator. If you stick to these steps and practice them continuously, then you will soon be able to learn and even master the art of effective communication. If you are a complete beginner who is just starting out, then do not expect to be able to master the following steps quickly and easily. But, if you persist in your practice, then these steps will get easier over time. Soon, they will become second nature to you. Allow these steps to become a part of you, and you will be able to do them smoothly and naturally.

So, is effective communication for you? The answer is *yes*, and it is well within your reach. The secrets to learning the art of effective communication and conversation are revealed in the pages of this book. Just keep your determination strong, never stop learning, and keep on practicing. This book will give you the knowledge that you need; it is up to you to turn it into actual practice.

Why would anyone want to learn how to talk to people effectively? If you stop for a while and notice what is going on around you, it is easy to recognize that the "machinery" of how the world works is mainly based on how people talk with one another. Gone are the days when swords and steel had to do the talking. In the modern world, people just talk to set things in motion. Whether you are in a workplace environment, in school, or even just in the comfort of your home, it is talking with one another that connects people. It is also how ideas, feelings, and thoughts are usually expressed. Hence, if you learn how to talk to people effectively, then just imagine the benefits that you can enjoy. You will be able to express your ideas more accurately; you can even influence people with your words; you can be a better negotiator; you can make people open up to you; you can build good relationships with people, and so much more. The possibilities become limitless. This is because you will be able to talk and connect with people on a deeper level. And, as you may already know, once you establish this kind of connection with people, then chances are that you can work together mutually and more effectively. Talking effectively with people is probably one of the best things to experience in life, and it can also open lots of opportunities for you.

Chapter 2: The 7 Steps

#1 Prepare

Preparation can go a long way. In fact, if you have enough preparation, then you could almost guarantee being able to talk effectively. But, how do you prepare? This is where the problem usually is. Many people know the importance of doing preparation, but only a few are able to do *sufficient* preparation.

If you know that you will be talking with someone, the first step that you should do is to prepare for the meeting. Know as much about the person whom you will be talking to. Find out about his interests, if possible. Although communication is about voicing out your thoughts and ideas, an important part of effective communication is to know about the other person. This should be part of your preparation. This is like preparing for a date. This will ensure that you can keep the other person interested in conversing with you. By talking about the other person's interest, you can make the other person happy talking with you. A common mistake made by beginners is to prepare only for the things that they want to say, without making any preparation for meeting the other person. Take note that you are dealing with another human being and not just someone who will listen and receive whatever you want to say.

There are no hard and fast rules on how you should prepare. The manner and amount of preparation that you need will depend on the circumstances of the situation. So, for example, you will be meeting with a business tycoon. Find out and research what his business is all about. If he is engaged in the stock market, then try to learn interesting things about the stock market. Also learn the current trend and happenings in the stock market. One way to communicate effectively is to talk about something that the other person is interested in.

Another part of your preparation is to expect the topics and subtopics that will be brought up during the actual meeting. It is important for you to have a good understanding of the subject matter so that you can give insightful and meaningful opinions. If you do not have a good grasp of the subject matter, then it will be hard to communicate anything worthwhile to the other person. One of the things that you should keep in mind is that effective communicators have mastery or at least a respectable amount of knowledge of what they are talking about. Hence, subject mastery should be part of your preparation.

How do you know if you have prepared enough for the meeting? It is quite hard to tell if the amount of preparation that you have is already enough or not, because a conversation can lead to so many things. But, ideally, you should be able to discuss the subject matter easily and smoothly. If you reach a point that talking and discussing the details of a particular topic is easy for you to do, then you are more likely to be ready to engage in an actual conversation. Of course, this means having a good amount of knowledge, and this knowledge can come from your preparation. Thanks to the Internet, you always have an access to a vast network of information. This will allow you to do your research in the comfort of your home. You may also want to read books and talk with and interview experts on the subject. This way you will be able to gain as much information that you need. Knowledge is important because if you do not know the subject matter of a conversation well, then it will be difficult for you to say something good and meaningful about it.

Another part of preparation is the physical preparation. It is a good practice to dress properly for the occasion. If you know that you are properly dressed and look decent enough, then you will be more confident to face and talk with other people. Needless to say, you need to be confident when you talk. If you are not confident, then people will find it difficult to trust you and believe whatever you say. You do not have to dress formally except, of course, if the situation requires it. However, you should always look presentable.

Unfortunately, you will not always be given time to make preparations. There are times when you will just find yourself in a conversation without any prior preparation. In this case, you can rely on other techniques as revealed in this book in order to keep the conversation effective and interesting. Of course, being able to prepare is a good advantage, so be sure to make use of it whenever possible.

#2 Listen

It is worth noting that effective communication is a two-way process. Unfortunately, many peoples think communication is just about being the one who is talking. This is wrong. From time to time, you should also be the one who is on the receiving end. One of the most important elements of effective communication is listening. To be more specific, this refers to *active listening.* It is unfortunate that although the importance of listening is a common advice, many people still fail to observe it. Keep in mind that listening means so much more than just hearing the other person's voice. When you listen, you should *understand* what the other person is saying. Another advice is to react to what the other person tells you. Giving a response ensures the other person that you are attentive to him and that you understand what he is saying.

There are certain differences between listening and active listening. Most people only know how to listen but they do not do it actively. So, how do you do active listening? When you actively listen to a person, you do not just hear his words. You should also ask questions and make appropriate responses to what the other person is telling you. Asking questions and reacting ensure the other person that he has your attention and that you are able to follow his train of thoughts. This is active listening. Listening, on the other hand, simply refers to hearing what the other person is telling you. Unfortunately, most people just know how to listen and do not make the other person feel that attention that you are actually giving him. When you actively listen to another, it will tend to make him feel loved and understood. Try talking to someone who actively listens to every word you say and you will know just how comforting it is to have someone to just talk to even if you do not get any solution to a problem. Indeed, many people are not really looking for a solution; they just want to have someone who would sincerely listen to them, someone who would hear whatever they say without judging them. Surprisingly, although this may seem an easy thing to do, most people are too preoccupied to even listen to another human being. Most of the time if they know that they would not gain anything from the conversation, they would rather avoid meeting the person. This book teaches its readers to value the existence and life of another person. Do not forget that the best time to talk with people effectively is not when you have something important to say, but when people actually want to talk with someone — and that someone could be you.

Do not commit the common mistake of being too self-centered. You should also take the time to hear and listen to what the other person has to say. If you are not willing to listen then it would be better for you to just talk with yourself. Remember: True effective communication is a two-way process. Before you even talk to somebody, be sure that you are also ready to listen. Unfortunately, many people become sort of narcissistic when they engage in conversation. They are too concerned with themselves that they fail to hear what the other person is telling them. Keep in mind that if you want to be a good communicator, then you should be a good listener.

Is it important for the other person to know that you are listening to him? The answer is *yes*. A common mistake committed by lots of people is to listen to a person without making him feel that they can hear him out. Take note that the person would not know that you can understand him unless you make positive responses. If the other person feels that you are actively listening to him, then you will more easily gain his trust, and he will feel more comfortable opening up to you. However, if the person feels that you are not giving him enough attention, then it would be hard to make him open up to you. Soon, he will feel very uncomfortable and even feel insulted if you do not make him feel that you are listening to him. So, how do you assure the other person that you are actively listening to him? Of course, you will not tell him, "Hey, I am listening to you." Rather, you will make him feel that you are actually listening to him while he is talking to you. You can easily do this by observing some simple practices like making eye contact and asking follow-up questions. For example, if a person says, "I am sad." ask him why he is sad. You cannot always expect people to open up to you immediately. Most of the time, you first need to make them feel that you want to listen to them and that you are someone whom they can trust. Once they feel how sincere you are and once they are comfortable enough talking with you, then that is the time when they will be more open to you. As you can see, the art of effective communication is not just about expressing your thoughts and ideas clearly, but is also about helping other people to express their thoughts and feelings and to share them with you.

Everyone will tell you that making eye contact is important. But, what if you find it uncomfortable to look at a person's eyes as you talk/listen? A good way to solve this problem is too look at the edge of his eye. This way, it will seem as if you are staring right at him. Another trick is to stare at the bridge of his nose right between his eyes. Of course the best way would still be to get used to looking at a person's eyes when you talk. Just practice it with every person you interact with, and you will soon get used to it. If you are truly sincere and would like to listen to another person, looking at his eyes would come naturally. As they say, "The eyes are the windows to the window."

From time to time, you may have to deal with people who are simply hard to listen to. Usually, these people are those who talk too much and simply have difficulty in expressing themselves clearly. Worse, they tend to talk loudly. So, how do you deal with these people? The principle remains the same: You have to listen. Now, if you find it hard to listen to everything that they are saying because you know that much of the things they are talking about do not really matter, the key is simply to identify keywords. You have to be patient with these people. You may find it irritating to listen to everything that they say, so a good tip is to just identify the real issue and ignore the others. Once you know the main issue, then you can always make an appropriate response. Sad to say, there are some people who have to talk for minutes just to say something that can be expressed in a few seconds. Again, effective communication teaches you to be good and respectable at all times.

You should also realize and appreciate that listening is an act of love and/or kindness. When you listen to another, you give him your time and attention. This is the kind of sincerity that people want. Needless to say, when somebody talks with you, you should stop whatever it is that you are doing and put your focus on the person who is talking. This is also the time to make eye contact with the person to assure him that you are listening to him.

A common mistake is to think that the person you are talking to is looking for a solution to a problem. The truth is that most people who talk about their problems are not really looking for a solution, but are merely looking for someone who would listen to them and understand them. Of course, the way to do this is by listening to the person who has a problem. These people simply want to be heard and understood. Unfortunately, many of these people feel that they are alone in the world, and so having someone who could listen and understand them would make them feel less alone. As you can see, the art of listening is a very important skill that you should master. In fact, expert communicators agree that listening is more important, if not as important, as talking. It is also by listening actively that you will be able to know how to best respond to a person. The more that you listen and understand a person, the easier it will be to connect with him on a deeper level.

#3 Ask the right questions

Learning to ask the right questions is a vital element of effective communication. It is also by asking questions that you can get to expound and deepen the level of conversation. It directs the flow of the conversation. By asking questions, you also assure the other person that you are actively listening to him and that you are able to follow his thoughts. However, do not be like other people who ask questions just for the sake of asking. Rather, every question that you ask must serve some purpose. A good advice is to ask only responsive questions. These are the questions that will get the story forward and develop the flow of conversation. For example, if a person says, "I took the bar exams." Ask him how he prepared for the exams and how he feels about them. This will definitely give you lots of information that you can use to further develop the level of conversation. By asking questions, you do not just make the person feel that you are listening to him, but it also encourages a person to talk more and open up to you. Needless to say, you should ask questions in a natural and gentle manner, and do not make the other person feel as if he were in some kind of investigation.

By asking questions, you make the other person feel that you are open to whatever it is that he has to say. Once again, effective communication is not just about you expressing your own thoughts and opinions. More importantly, it is about being open to other people and listening to whatever they have to say. Do not worry; you will also get your time to talk and share your own opinions.

Asking questions is also an excellent way to understand the other person. You should understand that effective communication is founded upon mutual respect and understanding. You need to understand each other. From time to time, you may have to tackle a sensitive topic where you may share different and even conflicting views. When you use effective communication, you can still talk about such matters without sacrificing peace and harmony between/among the parties. As the saying goes, "You can agree to disagree without sounding disagreeable." When you ask questions, you should also be ready to face answers that you may find unacceptable, but you need to learn to respect the other person. If you cannot respect a certain view or opinion, at least respect the other party as a person. After all, you are never obliged to adapt the same mindset or viewpoint. Indeed, from time to time, it is also important to appreciate the beauty in diversity.

Asking questions is one thing, asking the *right* questions is another. Expert communicators make sure to ask only the questions that will help develop a conversation. When you ask a question, that is the time when the other person will be expected to open up and share with you something, depending on your question. Be careful with the questions that you ask. Do not ask questions that would insult or offend the other person. If he feels that you are insulting him with your question then he will be more defensive, which will prevent you from having a meaningful conversation.

Most of the time, you only have to help the other person open up to you by asking him questions. For example, if a person says that he attended an event, ask him about the event. He will then tell you details about it. If you want to know more, then ask him more specific questions based on the information that he has also revealed to you. Simply stated, you only have to guide the person to share with you the whole story by asking him questions. This is the beauty of asking questions: You get to know more about the other person, and all that you need to do is ask.

#4 Share

Talking is sharing. Effective communication is about sharing and expressing yourself to people. Of course, you are expected to share something that the other person will like or at least find interesting.

But, what can you share? Every person has a story to tell. If not a story, then ideas, thoughts, opinions, and feelings that they can share with the world. Simply put, there is always something that you can share. The good thing about this is that you can share almost anything and everything that you want. However, effective communication is not just about sharing, but sharing something that the other person can also relate and connect to.

Do not underestimate the power of telling a good story. As they say, "Ideas come and go; stories stay." Sometimes it is most effective to tell whatever it is that you want to say in a narrative format. Stories usually have a way of expressing ideas more clearly. There is also power in stories that makes them hard to forget. Hence, you might want to use some storytelling when communicating effectively.

When you engage in a conversation, you should also expect for the other person to share something with you. You will have to take turns as to who will be the sender and the receiver, especially when telling a story. Do not worry; in every effective communication both or all parties will be given the chance the talk and share something. This is one of the things that set apart effective communication from just any other form of communication. Usually, when people think of the word *communication*, they only understand it to be a one-way process where you just have to talk whatever is on your mind. Worse, people usually do this carelessly without being careful of their choice of words. Hence, it is easy to understand why many people are not effective communicators.

When you share, you should also be open to feedbacks. After sharing something, you will most likely get a response from the receiver. Now, whatever response you get, remind yourself to remain calm and respectful. If you come to think of it, although it may seem that how a person responds is outside of your control, you actually have some control over it. This is because you can expect how a statement or story that you share would make the other person think or feel about it. For example, if you mention your recent success in life, then you can expect for your friend to be happy for you. Hence, before you share something, it is a good practice to pause for a moment and reflect how it would appear to the person with whom you want to tell it.

Effective communication aims to be able to build an environment and relationship based on trust where the parties are free to share everything with each other. This is one of the best things about learning effective communication. It also takes into account the relationship that you build with the other person. It is not just about expressing an idea, feeling, or thought. It also focuses on building good relationships.

When you share, especially when you share your weakness, it makes the other person feel that you can be trusted since you are the one who even reveal your vulnerability. People like honesty and openness. The only reason that usually prevents them for being open is because of some trust issue. But, if you take the initiative and be the one to remove your own walls and share, you can rest assured that it will be appreciated. Most of the time, it will make the other party feel that you are someone whom he can trust and rely on. Needless to say, you also have to be careful with what you share, especially if it is related to business or your profession.

Sharing can be a wonderful experience, especially if you know that the other person is sincere about it. When you share something, you give and entrust a part of you to another. In the same way, when a person shares something with you, you also receive something from him, perhaps an information, a secret, a story, or otherwise. The point is that when a person shares something, a connection is made. Now, it is only how you handle and respond to it which will determine if the connection is still worth having or not. Effective communicators know that value of sharing and respect whatever they receive from other people. Since they respect people regardless of their views, people also respect them. Never forget that effective communication is about building a good relationship. There is no reason to argue with one another. You only have to share and listen, and be respectful at all times.

The moment that you decide to talk to another, it is also a decision to finally be open to another human being. A common obstacle that prevents people from sharing or opening up to another is shyness. You need to understand that you should not allow shyness to prevent you from connecting with another person. Remember: As long as you are honest, then you do not have to be shy. If you focus on being shy, then you only make it stronger. If you continuously allow shyness to prevent you from having a good conversation, then you will not be able to experience the beauty of connecting with another person. Also, if you really feel uncontrollably shy, just remember that you are talking to just another human being. Feeling shy is normal. The best way to overcome shyness is by exposing yourself to more people. Soon, you will get used to it, and you will be more confident.

#5 Gestures

"Actions speak louder than words." Learn to use gestures effectively. Another thing that you should learn is how to read gestures. Also learn to understand facial expressions. Learning to use the right gestures is a good way to better illustrate your point, as well as to keep the conversation alive and interesting. Learning to read gestures will allow you to understand another person more clearly even before he says a word, or even when he says something that totally contradicts the truth. Gestures would reveal to you information that otherwise may be hidden from you. In fact, many people do not even realize how much information they share with others simply from their gestures. If you learn to understand the meaning behind the gestures, then you may be able to start reading people like a book. This means being more understanding of them.

It is also worth noting that not all gestures may signify a clear meaning. For example, some people associate a certain movement to mean that the person is lying. However, just because you see another person doing it does not mean that the said person is lying. This is where reading gestures can be tricky. However, it is still beneficial to know and understand the different gestures and their possible meanings. Although you cannot rely solely on gestures in understanding people, they can, nonetheless, still give you good insights not just about the subject matter of the conversation but also about the person with whom you are talking to.

One of the effective communicators who used gestures was Adolf Hitler. Yes, even Hitler knew the power of gestures that he studied his own gestures and learned to apply them more effectively. Feel free to learn the different gestures, as well as how you can apply them. There are helpful gestures that you can easily learn and use. These gestures can help you to illustrate a point more effectively and make the conversation more interesting. Of course, gestures alone are not enough. You should also communicate something that has meaning and value.

Learning to use gestures is a good way to be an effective communicator as it will also allow you to express your idea more clearly. It is also worth noting that gestures come naturally. However, there are those that have been used by humanity for ages that people associate them with a corresponding meaning. For example, closing your arms signify that you are taking a defensive position. However, some people simply like to cross their arms even for no reason. Hence, it is also good to know the meaning behind the gestures, so that you can correctly avoid using certain gestures that may cause misunderstanding and confusion, as well as to be able to get information from people even without talking directly to them. This will allow you to be able to understand people more effectively.

It can be stressing that gestures do not always mean what people say that they signify, hence, just because a person looks away after you ask him a question does not always mean that he is lying to you. Some people simply respond differently from the normal. A good way to know if your understanding of a certain gesture is correct or not is by testing it. After some time, you will get used to this to the point that you can tell if a specific gesture really intends to convey the meaning that has been associated with it or simply just a coincidence. This is something that comes with practice. One thing is sure: Learning about gestures can get you one step ahead of the conversation. If your job is something that requires convincing people and/or something that requires you to understand other people more completely, then learning to read gestures is something that should be in your arsenal. Although reading gestures is not always 100% accurate, it can, nonetheless, give you valuable insights which can be helpful.

Using gestures is also an excellent way to keep the conversation alive and interesting. Imagine talking to someone who does nothing but talk without using any gesture. Soon enough, you will surely get bored listening to him even if he is saying something interesting. Proper use of gestures can add action to the conversation, which will give it more life.

A common mistake is to use the same gesture over and over again. Most people who are not aware of effective communication simply allow themselves to use gestures unconsciously. Although gestures usually just happen even if you do not give it any thought, you will most likely be using the same gesture over and over again if you just allow it to express itself naturally. When this happens, your movement can look monotonous, and this may not look good to the person who is listening to you. Therefore, it is also a good advice for you to know the different gestures and then try to use them when you talk. A good way to practice with gestures is to watch yourself in the mirror as you talk. Pay attention to how you move and the gestures that you make. Also take note of your facial expressions, as well as how you project yourself. Make sure to use gestures naturally. Forcing to use a certain gesture may make you look awkward, so be sure to apply every gesture smoothly and in accordance with the thought or emotion that you are trying to convey.

#6 Trust

You need to remember that effective communication is based on trust. If the person you are talking with trusts you enough, then he will be more open to you. The more open and honest a conversation is, the more meaningful it will be. But, how do you make people trust you? You should understand that effective communication does not use deception. It is not about manipulating the other person. Rather, effective communication creates a bond of trust and confidence because you are worthy of being trusted. The key to this is sincerity. Unfortunately, some people think that they have to use tricks, deception, and lies to be an effective communicator. This is not true. In fact, although such lies may work to your advantage for some time, they will soon ruin your reputation in the long run. Hence, your focus should be on building a good relationship with people.

If you pay attention to the techniques in this book, as well as in other books, you will notice that the techniques are not really out of the ordinary, such as making eye contact, asking questions, and others. They are simply what a kind, decent, and sincere person would do if engaged in a conversation with someone whom he deeply cares about. Effective communication makes you to be that person. This is one of the reasons why learning to communicate effectively can change a person. The art of effective communication teaches one how to act as a gentleman or a kind and loving person.

It is usual for people to have walls as a form of defensive mechanism. After all, these days, it is hard to find people whom you can trust completely. However, these walls can be a barrier to an effective communication. You probably recognized these walls when you talk to someone who seems very reserved and does not open up to you. When this happens, the tendency is for you to be the one to do all the talking, which is not good. Although it is still considered communication, it is not *effective* communication. Again, communication is a two-way process. So, how do you make such kind of people to open up to you? An effective way is to show the person that it is okay to bring down his/her walls. To do this, you have to take the initiative and bring down your own walls to show the person that it is safe not to have any defenses. Show him your own vulnerability. In other words, trust the other person, and show him that you trust him. Most of the time, when you do this, the other person will appreciate your efforts and initiative and will start to lower his walls and begin to open up to you as well. When this happens, you can now engage in a more meaningful conversation.

When people study how to communicate with people more effectively, they often focus on themselves, specifically on how to express their thoughts and ideas more effectively. Although this is part of effective communication, the process does not end there. Unfortunately, they fail to realize that the person they are talking to are not effective communicators. Hence, instead of just focusing on yourself and what you have to say, you can have a more meaningful conversation by also helping the other person in expressing his thoughts, feelings, and ideas. When a person feels that it is easy and comfortable talking with you, then you will be able to gain his trust.

In our world today full of shrewd people who seek only for their own gain, it is not easy to find someone with whom you can talk about everything and feel good for doing so. This book teaches you how to be that person, and how you can turn a simple conversation into something that is meaningful and memorable.

Trust is important. If you have bad intentions, then this book is not for you. To make the other person trust you, then you should be worthy of being trusted. Usually, a good way to show the other person your own vulnerability is by showing him your own weaknesses. Normally, people will tend to be more open once they know that you are already being open to them. So, take the initiative and the risk and bring down your own walls first. Sometimes in order to be trusted, you need to be the first one to trust someone.

It is also important not to break a person's trust. Hence, be sure to always be true to your words and do not resort to any falsehood. Also, if a person has entrusted you with a secret, make sure to keep it a secret forever. Trust, once broken, is almost impossible to restore. Take very good care of it.

#7 Be more connected

This is the part where you deepen the level of conversation and get more connected. Normally, this part happens on its own and is simply about observing the aforesaid techniques continuously. This is mainly about building a stronger relationship. Talking to a person does not usually happen just once. If you get to feel comfortable with each other, then you will most likely meet up again and talk some more. In fact, if you come to think of it, the relationships in the world share the very same activity: talking. It is by talking with one another that people negotiate things. It is also how people share thoughts and ideas on a regular basis. Hence, if you want to be more connected, then it would mean having more conversations with the same person or persons. This is simply how the world works: People get connected by talking with one another.

When you talk with people, a suggested approach is to consider every person that you talk to as special. It does not matter whether you are talking with your boss at work, a colleague, friend, spouse, or any one at all. The key is to see everyone as special and to treat them in a special way. Sadly, people have already forgotten just how meaningful talking should be. This is exactly why learning how to talk effectively is important, especially in today's world where people easily take things for granted.

It is important for you to realize what it really means to *talk*. If done with sincerity and kindness, talking creates a connection that can go beyond the physical. Have you experienced having a soulful connection with someone? This can be achieved through effective communication. Once people trust each other and become more open, other positive energies like love, kindness, hope, and even happiness, can be channeled through talking — and this can create a truly meaningful and powerful bond.

Repeated meetings and talks can make a bond or relationship much stronger. Of course, you are expected to continuously apply the techniques as revealed in this book. As you can see by now, these techniques are not something that you apply today and forget tomorrow. Rather, they become *you*. Perhaps this is one of the reasons why some people find it hard to communicate effectively: They are not sincere enough to do it. To talk effectively, you cannot just fake being sincere or listening to people. You should be truly sincere and actually listen to whatever they tell you. This is something that you cannot just act out intentionally. If you are not sincere enough, then the other person will most likely feel your insincerity. How can you look at a person in the eyes and say that you care if you do not feel like caring at all? Hence, if you want to turn yourself into an effective communicator, you should also improve yourself as a person. Self-improvement is part of the process.

The more connected you are to a person, the more the communication will deepen. This is another reason why you should not fake being sincere; it is because it would not last long. If you are not true enough, then the other person will soon recognize it. You should also realize that even if you talk effectively, it does not guarantee that anyone would love to talk with you. After all, talking effectively does not mean pleasing or entertaining everyone whom you talk with. Hence, do not expect for people to flock around you and like you for being an effective communicator. Rather, just know that by learning these techniques, you will be able to connect more intimately with people, and that this art of talking would make you a better human being.

Chapter 3: Best Practices

Learn from the experts

When learning to communicate effectively, you will most likely try to learn from experts who claim to have mastered the art of effective communication. Feel free to visit their blogs and read their books on the subject. However, just be careful, because not everyone who claims to be an expert in effective communication is a real expert. In today's world, it is fairly easy to promote one's self as an expert in anything. Therefore, take whatever you read or hear with a grain of salt. The best way to know if a certain technique actually works is by testing it.

Although it is good to learn from experts, it is strongly suggested that you do not depend on them completely. Do not forget that effective communication is an art. Therefore, you should also develop your own style of conversing with people.

It is also a good idea to closely study how the real experts communicate. For example, play a certain video and pay attention to how an expert talks, his gestures, how he uses pauses, tone of voice, and others.

A good way to learn from experts is by watching their videos. You might want to try YouTube for this. Pay attention to how these "experts" talk and get a message across very clearly. It is also advised that you videos of famous orators and observe how they deliver their message powerfully. Take note of their choice of words, voice, posture and gestures, as well as the way that they project themselves to the audience. Orators are usually great communicators who are able to deliver a message powerfully. Of course, their techniques may not always be applicable to a day-to-day conversation, but you can still learn from them, especially from the way they use words to express their thoughts and emotions.

Find your voice

You need to find your voice as early as possible. Usually, a beginner will try to imitate how an expert talks. This is not a good approach. The thing is that no matter how hard you try, you cannot completely duplicate another person's style of talking with people. Instead, what you should do is to develop your own style by using your own voice.

Finding your own voice takes trial and error. Many times it is knowing what your voice *is not* that will lead you to find the voice that is truly your own. Every person has his or her own voice. Take note that this does not refer to your literal *voice*, but is rather something about the way you connect with other people. It is also something that you develop as you continue to practice effective communication.

Effective communication is an art. There are many ways to apply the same techniques. To help you find your voice, you can try to adapt different styles of communicating and see which one best suits your personality. The best way to know your unique voice is to just be yourself. Do not think about being successful or being an effective communicator. Simply be yourself and talk naturally. Of course, this does not mean that you should be careless in your approach. However, it should be noted that aside from applying the techniques, it is also important to be yourself when you talk.

Talk clearly

When you talk, make sure that you pronounce all the words clearly. Some people tend to "eat" their words or talk too fast. Help the receiver to understand your message by conveying it in a clear and easy-to-understand manner. A good advice to be able to talk more clearly is to talk slowly and make sure that you pronounce all the words clearly and correctly. Also, be as concise as possible. Avoid using statements that are too wordy. Avoid unnecessary words and go straight to the point.

If you have problems with stammering, then a good way to avoid or at least lessen such problem is by talking more slowly. Now, it takes practice to do this, especially if you are used to talking too fast. However, this is something that you can easily learn with continuous practice. The key is to always remind yourself to talk clearly. A common mistake is only to practice it when you need it. What you should do is to make it a part of your day-to-day conversations. Keep in mind that how you talk in your day-to-day conversations will most likely be the way you talk when you attend meetings, events, and others. Also, effective communication embraces all forms of conversations, so it is only right that you apply the techniques every time you engage in any conversation, including the usual day-to-day talks that you engage in.

You should also learn how to regulate your voice. Learn when to use a high tone and a low tone, also learn when to whisper. If you observe expert communicators, you will notice how they play with their voice and use it strategically. They project their voice powerfully and deliver the message that they want to get across very clearly. Also, being too monotonous can be boring, so regulate your voice and avoid following a single rhythm.

Be flexible

Effective communication requires one to be flexible enough. Hence, it does not have any fixed rule to follow. How you approach a subject will most likely depend on the circumstances of a situation. It is also worth noting that you cannot always expect to talk with someone who shares the same view as you have. Hence, you should also be flexible enough to welcome other points of view.

Depending on the person with whom you are talking to, you may also have to adjust how you talk from time to time. This is not about being untrue to yourself, but merely for the sake of being more effective. After all, you cannot expect for everyone to respond in the same way. If a certain technique does not work on a certain person, then you might want to try another technique in its place.

Being flexible also refers to the ability of controlling yourself. Sometimes you may have to control your reaction and choice of words. Do not forget that part of effective communication is learning how to make the other person feel more respected and comfortable. Of course, being flexible does not mean that you should aim to please the other person. It bears stressing that you are not obliged in any way to please the other person. There is a difference between pleasing another person and allowing him to be more comfortable with you.

Not everyone will respond to you the way that you expect or would want them to. You will also definitely meet people who are very hard to predict, and some would even be rude to you. You should be flexible enough to handle all these types of people. This may be hard for beginners, but if you practice enough, then you will soon be able to handle any kind of conversation and people. Talking to people is an art. There is no rule as to how you should respond or react, and there is also no rule as to what you should tell the other person. You are always free to express yourself. Unfortunately, many people are not good at expressing themselves. You should be flexible enough to deal with such kind of people. You may have to be more patient and make some adjustments just to talk with them effectively. Sometimes the art of talking is like a dance where you also need to make some adjustments in order to move harmoniously with another. There is strict rule that will work for all occasions. This is why you need to find your own voice and set your rhythm.

Be respectful

Be respectful at all times. No matter what happens, never allow your temper or emotion to control the conversation. You should always stay calm and relaxed. A good characteristic of any effective communicator is the respect with which he carries himself. By being respectful, the other person will also feel that he should respect you. Now, it is easy to show respect if you are talking to someone who is very kind and nice. But, what if you find yourself dealing with a difficult person, or a person who only wants to get into a debate with you? In such instances, you may find your temper and patience being put the test. During such time, you should remain respectful. Never succumb to anger. As the saying goes, "Always be a gentleman. Not because the other person is a gentleman, but because you are."

Respect is very important to any relationship, even in a conversation of any kind. No matter how the other person treats you, be sure to treat him kindly. Sometimes it is by respecting other people that they will learn how to respect you. Respect can earn respect.

Have an open mind

It is important for you to keep an open mind when you engage in a conversation. When you converse with a person, you may encounter strange and even contradicting ideas. You get to brainstorm ideas with each other. If you do not have an open mind, then some of the ideas may seem very wrong and revolting. But, if you keep an open mind, then you can have a healthy conversation with anyone. Take note that you do not need to convince the other person to adapt your way of thinking. In the same way, you are not expected to agree with everything that the other person is saying. You are always free to disagree. Just remember to express your disagreement politely and respectfully. You need to understand that you disagree with a certain view or opinion but not necessarily with the person. Hence, you can always have respect for a person despite his contradicting and even erroneous views. Good communicators know that a person is not always what he says when he talks. In fact, many people are not good at expressing themselves. Therefore, it is very important for you to keep an open mind at all times. By having an open mind, you will also be more open to new and interesting ideas. People also like talking to someone who has an open mind. They want to open up to people whom they know will not judge them no matter what they say. This is another important lesson to remember: Having an open mind means not judging a person no matter what he tells you. Instead, what you should do is to try to understand more the other person. You are not there to judge, but to listen. If you cannot listen and sympathize with another, then perhaps it would be better if you do not engage in a conversation. Again, effective communication is not just about you. It is two-way process. Just as there is a time for you to talk, there is also a time for you to listen.

Have a sense of humor

Learn to laugh — laugh even at yourself and your mistakes. If you notice expert communicators, they usually add some humor to their talks. A humor can release some tension and make people feel more comfortable. Therefore, it is a good practice to use some humor from time to time. However, just be sure to use a humor whenever it is proper. Using humor can make a serious conversation to seem lighter. However, keep in mind that there are also times when the setting is completely serious without any place to drop some humor. Make sure to observe proper timing; otherwise, a humor might be taken out of context and be received as an insult.

Adding some humor is not always an easy thing to do. There is also no assurance that the other person will like it. Hence, if you notice that the person whom you are talking to is trying his best to humor you, show your appreciation for his efforts. Of course, you should also do the same favor and try to use a little humor in your conversation. Also, engaging in a very serious conversation for hours can be very boring and can even make you feel exhausted easily. A good humor, especially when followed by a good laugh, can make you feel less stressed and more comfortable. Therefore, whenever possible, try to use some humor in your conversations.

Learn to use pauses

A pause can be a powerful tool in effective communication. A pause can draw more attention, arouse interest, or it can also give emphasis to something. One of the effective communicators who used a pause properly was Adolf Hitler. Hitler used to pause for few seconds before starting his speech. A pause draws attention, and you will be sure that you have all the attention and focus of the audience the moment you start talking. A pause can also be used to build up the suspense and make the conversation more interesting.

You should remember to use pauses wisely and sparingly. Using too many pauses may not be a good idea; therefore, only use it when you have a clear purpose for doing so. If it does not serve a good purpose, then do not apply it.

Focus on the relationship

You need to realize that talking to people is about building a good relationship. It means so much more than just getting a message across or listening to what the other person has to say. Focus on relationship-building. The more that you are able to build a good relationship, the better the conversation will be.

A common mistake is focusing more on the gain that you expect to get from the conversation. This is true, especially when you attend business meetings. Of course, you will not sacrifice the interest of your business. But, you also need to be cautious of projecting an image of being too greedy. People will find it hard to trust you if they notice that you only care about your own interest.

An effective way to build a good relationship is to focus on the interest of the other person. If you talk about something that the other person is interested in, then you will definitely capture his interest, and he will most likely enjoy talking with you. It is not a surprise that business meetings usually end up with talks about golf, cars, and others. When this happens, friendship starts to develop, and a more meaningful relationship takes shape. Also, when you do this, people will usually appreciate it and tend to be more open and friendly.

Continuous practice

Truly learning effective communication takes more than just reading books and theories about it. In order to become an effective communicator, you need to take positive actions and engage in continuous practice. As already stated, you should apply the techniques of effective communication even in your day-to-day conversations. Remember that every conversation you have is another opportunity to apply and improve your communication skills. After some time, all the techniques and habits of effective communication will be a part of who you are as a person. By then, you will realize that communicating effectively is not a difficult task. By improving your character, you also improve your level of communication. In a way, it can be said that learning how to communicate effectively is about learning to become a better person. This is one of the reasons why learning to become a better and effective communicator is highly beneficial. It also improves you as a person. Not to mention, those who can communicate effectively are usually those who get rewarded since they are the ones who excel at what they do.

You cannot just turn into an expert communicator overnight. Even if you read all the books about talking to people, you still need to spend time and efforts to actually learn the techniques. Of course, the only way to learn them is by active and continuous application.

For starters, it is advised that you focus on learning the techniques one at a time. Hence, you might want to focus on active listening before moving on to other techniques and tips. As you improve and get used to the process of effective communication, you can then apply two or more techniques at the same time. Of course, once you get good at this, you should soon be able to use all the techniques at once and handle any kind of conversation effectively and confidently. Speaking about confidence, it is also an important ingredient of effective communication. The more that you practice, the more confident you will be. Unfortunately, many people who try to learn how to talk effectively do not practice enough. Keep this in mind: Actual practice is very important. You need to try to apply the techniques regularly. Also, do not just wait for people to come and talk to you. You should take the initiative and be more social and talk to people. For purpose of practicing the techniques, it is strongly suggested that you make sure to talk to at least one person everyday and be sure to apply the techniques in this book. Do not be discouraged if you are not able to execute them properly. Practice makes perfect, so spend more time practicing the teachings in this book. Soon, you will get used to it and these techniques will be second nature to you that you would not even have to think about them. Instead, they will be a habit that becomes a natural part of who you are. If you watch the videos of expert communicators, you will notice that they are always very relaxed. This is because they do not even think about the techniques. This is because once you reach that level, these techniques are no longer considered techniques but are already a part of who you are as a person. Again, it bears stressing that learning to talk effectively can be a life-changing journey that is full of positive changes.

Conclusion

Thanks for making it through to the end of this book. I hope it was informative and able to provide you with all of the tools you need to achieve your goals whatever they may be.

The next step is to apply everything that you have learned. Learning to talk to people effectively requires continuous practice. It is worth remembering that talking to people is something that is innate in human beings. Hence, do not see the techniques in this book as something difficult to do. Take note that you already have all these skills; you simply have to develop them. If you are just starting out, you may expect to have some difficulty in applying the techniques and tips in this book. This is normal, so do not be discouraged. Just persist in your practice, and you will soon notice some improvements. Learning to communicate more effectively is just like learning any other new skill. Even if you have all the instructions that you may need, it will still take and practice before you can completely learn how to use the techniques properly.

As you may have already noticed by now, there is really no secret to effective communication. It is only about being and acting more human and knowing that you are connecting with another human being. It is by realizing this truth that makes the activity of talking meaningful and valuable. When you talk, you open yourself up to people. Depending on the quality of the words that you say, you either send positive or negative energy out into the world. In the same manner, when you are the receiver and listens to another, you receive whatever the other person is opening up to you. The process of communication is a beautiful exchange that takes place between two or more human beings.

It is worth noting that you should not limit yourself to the techniques in this book, as well as other books on the same subject. Talking effectively to people is an art; therefore, do not let any teaching to put limitation as to how talking should be. Feel free to modify the techniques and even come up with your own set of techniques. Since talking can be considered an art, use it in a way that you express yourself more beautifully and effectively.

As you learn and apply the techniques of effective communication, you will notice some positive changes in your life. Most likely, you will notice how people respond more favorably when you talk to them effectively. You may even make new friends and show excellence in what you do. More importantly, learning how to talk effectively will make you more human and make you conscious of the beauty that comes with connecting to another human being. Unfortunately, since people talk and talk every day, many tend to take things for granted that they fail to see how wonderful it is to connect and talk with another human being. Learning to talk effectively to people will remind you of what truly matters and make you a better human being.

There is joy in being able to talk effectively to people. Indeed, this is a "skill" that is worth learning. By now, you should already have a good foundation and understanding of how to talk to people effectively. Feel free to review the techniques and even come up with your own. More importantly, be sure to apply your knowledge. Effective communication requires continuous practice. Stop being shy or worrying; it is time for you to enjoy connecting with another soul: Talk and connect with another human being.

HOW TO
ASK QUESTIONS
THE RIGHT WAY

The Only 7 Steps You Need to Master
Inquiry Communication Skills, Solving Problems
and Getting the Right Answers Today

DEAN MACK

BOOK 2: HOW TO ASK QUESTIONS

THE RIGHT WAY

The Only 7 Steps You Need to Master Inquiry Communication Skills, Solving Problems and Getting the Right Answers Today

Dean Mack

This document is geared towards providing exact and reliable information in regards to the topic and issue covered. The publication is sold with the idea that the publisher is not required to render accounting, officially permitted, or otherwise, qualified services. If advice is necessary, legal or professional, a practiced individual in the profession should be ordered.

From a Declaration of Principles which was accepted and approved equally by a Committee of the American Bar Association and a Committee of Publishers and Associations.

In no way is it legal to reproduce, duplicate, or transmit any part of this document in either electronic means or in printed format. Recording of this publication is strictly prohibited and any storage of this document is not allowed unless with written permission from the publisher. All rights reserved.

The information provided herein is stated to be truthful and consistent, in that any liability, in terms of inattention or otherwise, by any usage or abuse of any policies, processes, or directions contained within is the solitary and utter responsibility of the recipient reader. Under no circumstances will any legal responsibility or blame be held against the publisher for any reparation, damages, or monetary loss due to the information herein, either directly or indirectly.

Respective authors own all copyrights not held by the publisher.

The information herein is offered for informational purposes solely, and is universal as so. The presentation of the information is without contract or any type of guarantee assurance.

The trademarks that are used are without any consent, and the publication of the trademark is without permission or backing by the trademark owner. All trademarks and brands within this book are for clarifying purposes only and are the owned by the owners themselves, not affiliated with this document.

Table of Contents

Introduction

I want to thank you and congratulate you for purchasing the book, *"How to Ask Questions: The Right Way"*

This book contains proven steps and strategies on how to develop effective communication skills so that you can ask effective questions that will provide you with the important information which you are seeking. Asking questions is a form of communication that anyone can do, even toddlers seem to be able to ask questions nonstop! However, asking questions thoughtfully and respectfully can take some practice. The sole guide of this book is to provide you with the information and tips necessary for you to become a master at effectively asking intelligent questions.

Sometimes the way in which we ask questions can actually be counterproductive to our information goals. Think of the last time that you asked another individual a question, and they provided you with information that was either slightly or completely off topic. These kinds of misunderstandings often happen in conversations where someone is seeking specific information or asking multiple questions, and these misunderstandings can be very time consuming and frustrating. This book aims to act as a communication guide so that you can ask questions effectively and try to avoid these misunderstandings all together!

I hope you enjoy it!

Chapter 1: Plan Ahead

Asking questions is very beneficial. Not only it can satisfy our curiosity and give us more knowledge, but it can also help us start a meaningful discussion with someone. To start a conversation, a simple "hello" or handshake is good. But some find it very old-school. Many find asking simple questions to be an effective way of starting a good talk. However, many people do not have the strength to do so probably because they do not have the courage to, or because they do not know where to start. Thus, resulting to poor communication.

One of the main things that contribute to poor communication is an individual's inability to prepare properly. When you find that you need to have a serious or lengthy conversation with someone else, it is important that you first adequately prepare for the conversation that will take place. If you go up to the other individual to ask them questions without being prepared, you will likely not get the answers that you need, and you may be left with more questions than you had before. In planning for a conversation with another individual, be sure to plan which questions you need to ask. Below we have listed several tips that can help you plan for your upcoming conversation.

List

Creating a list is a great way to determine what questions you would like to ask during the upcoming conversation. How many times have you asked another individual a question, only to find that you were left with new questions that you had not previously considered when the conversation was over? Of course, it is impossible to know all questions about a conversation ahead of time, but creating a list can help you consider the bulk of possible questions to ask. By creating a list of possible questions to ask, you may also find that you already know some of the answers. Sometimes we simply need to "think out loud" to realize that we know more about a given topic than we had originally thought. When creating a list of questions which you intend to ask to make sure that you rank them by importance. On your question outline, it is also a good idea to keep follow up questions positioned directly beneath the questions which they need to follow so that you do not forget to ask these questions during your conversation. Once you have completed a full list of possible questions (and their follow up questions), you will be able to determine which questions are most important and place them higher up on your priority list for the conversation. Creating a list of your questions will also allow you the chance to place them in an order which makes sense so that you do not confuse the other individual, thus avoiding a possible misunderstanding which could be counterproductive to your information goals.

Roleplay

Roleplaying is another great way to prepare yourself for a time when you need to gain information from another individual by asking questions. Begin by asking yourself the first question that you plan to ask the other individual, then determine what the possible responses to this question could be. Based on these responses, think of what follow up questions you may want to ask to continue collecting necessary information. Continue this pattern until you are sure that you have been able to think of the majority of questions that you could need to ask in your upcoming conversation. When roleplaying possible questions and answers, be sure to take into account the other individuals emotions. Emotions can largely affect the type of information that you are given in response to your questions, especially if the topic is the least bit controversial or relies on the other person reflecting on past experiences to answer your questions. Roleplaying gives you the chance to think of questions ahead of time-based on possible responses to your previous questions so that you can be sure the conversation ends only after you have gathered all of the pertinent information.

Determine Goals

A great way to prepare for a conversation with another individual in which you will need to ask them multiple questions is to create an outline of your information goals. Try to decide well ahead of time what your goal for the conversation is. What questions do you need to ask? What specific information do you need to obtain? Are there any follow-up questions to your original questions that you may want to consider ahead of time? And lastly, do you have the necessary information to answer any questions that may be asked to you by the individual in question? Determining your information goals ahead of time will greatly help you to become prepared for your upcoming conversation. Appropriate goal setting is a very important practice when it comes to mastering communication skills. If you set unrealistic goals for yourself, you are not very likely to successfully achieve them. If you do not successfully achieve your goals, you will likely feel disappointed in your failure and as a result feel a greater temptation to quit working towards your goals. Joe Friel (former coach of Olympic triathlon athlete Ryan Bolton) validates the importance of appropriate goal setting in making that success a reality with his quote "A dream becomes a goal when you create a plan, and a reality only when you fully commit to it." As stated in Friel's quote, there are multiple steps involved in successfully achieving any goal. To successfully achieve a goal, you must first create a specific goal, create a plan of how you plan to achieve that goal, and commit the time and effort required to make that goal a reality.

When setting goals for yourself, it is important to make sure that your goals are specific. General goals are more difficult to obtain. Consider this as an example: successfully achieving the general goal of "I want to be better at talking to people" is a lot harder to achieve than the specific goal of "I want to have four meaningful conversations with people this month." A general goal leaves a lot of open-ended questions that, left unanswered, can actually be counterproductive in achieving your goal. By setting too general a goal, you are setting yourself up for failure which may make it much harder to master communication skills and ask questions effectively.

Once you have set a specific goal for yourself, make a realistic timeline for achieving your goal. It is also a good idea to share your goals with another person. If the only person who knows about your goal is yourself, it bears very little weight and has no real consequence to you not achieving it. If you tell a friend or family member about your goal, they are likely to ask you how the achievement of this goal is going after some time (which will motivate you to continue working hard towards your goal). This also works as a way to ensure you continuously work towards your goal: the failure to achieve your goal will be harder to swallow if you have to admit it to someone other than yourself, and you will likely work harder to achieve your goal to avoid having to admit failure to a close friend or family member.

Chapter 2: Which Questions to Ask & How to Ask Them Logically

Before entering a conversation with another individual with the goal of asking various questions in mind, be sure to first determine which questions you need to ask. Narrow down the list of possible questions to only those questions which are essential to achieving your information goals, and try to also ask only one question at a time. Knowing how to word the necessary questions can also play a vital role in obtaining the pertinent information which you are seeking.

Ask Only Necessary Questions

When your goal for a conversation is to gain specific information, it is important that you ask only important questions. When planning the questions that you will ask in a conversation, ask yourself what the possible responses to that question are and is that information necessary to achieve your information goals? A good way to weed out unnecessary questions is to begin with your information goals and decide which question can best be used to obtain that information. For example, if you information goal is to find out _how many car accidents are caused by alcohol intoxication each month_ you could first ask _how many car accidents were reported last month_ and then follow up with the questions _how many of those accidents were related to alcohol consumption?_ Asking only the necessary questions will help you to be sure you are obtaining only the necessary information as well: if you are not asking unnecessary questions, you should not receive any answers which are irrelevant to obtaining your information goals. Consider this as well, your time or the other individual's patience may be limited so you must choose which questions you are going to ask wisely and make the most of the time you are given. If you only have 10 minutes to have a conversation with someone, you need to ask the right questions to gain all necessary information in that time frame. Also, if you are asking dozens of questions the person you are questioning may become frustrated, annoyed, or bored (and as a result may be unwilling to offer much useful information). By only asking questions that are necessary for achieving your information goals, you will be utilizing your time wisely so that you receive the maximum benefit from the pending conversation.

Ask Only One Question at a Time

When you are having a conversation with another individual in which you are asking multiple questions, it is also extremely important that you only ask the individual a single question at a time. If you ask multiple questions at once, you are more likely to annoy or confuse the other person. By asking more than one question at a time, you also run the risk that the person answering your questions may not be able to keep up. If the individual in question cannot keep up with the rate at which you are asking questions, they are more likely to only half-answer your questions, or they may omit some answers to your questions to save on time or attempt to keep up. In choosing the necessary questions to ask, you will not feel like you have a tight time restriction and that will result in you being less likely to rush through the conversation by asking multiple questions at once. To gain the necessary information, take your time in asking questions and be sure that the other individual has fully answered the previous question before you attempt to ask them the next question. Spacing your questions out so that there is ample time between them is beneficial not only in making sure that the other person has finished answering their question, but the moment of silence may be uncomfortable for them which causes them to continue offering up more information in an attempt to answer your question in a more in-depth manner.

Choose Your Words

The way in which you word something could lead someone's mind to think you mean something completely different from what you originally intended. How many times have you been having a conversation with someone and found that your brain went off in a different direction because something that the other person said was poorly worded? For many of us, this is a fairly common occurrence. Make sure that when you are asking some individuals multiple questions that you choose your wording for these questions carefully. If your questions are poorly worded, there is a higher chance that you will receive incorrect information because the individual in question misunderstood what it was that you were really asking. Choosing your words carefully can also help to ensure that your questions probe the other individual to provide adequate and detailed answers (these answers will be great tools in achieving your information goals for the conversation). If you are fairly new to the topic in question, you can easily research common terminology for your topic online or by visiting a library or bookshop. Using terms specific to the topic at hand can help to ensure that no misunderstandings arise and will also help the other person to appreciate the work which you have already put in as an attempt to prepare for the conversation.

Ask Follow Up Questions

When you are asking specific questions to another individual, it can often be a good idea to have some follow up questions for the answers that they provide you with. Not all questions can be adequately asked when phrased as a single question, and some of the more lengthy or complex questions may be better off being separated into several smaller or simpler questions. Ask follow up questions such as where did you learn that, or why do you think that. These follow up questions will provide you with more detailed and in-depth answers to the questions which you have asked. Asking follow up questions can also be a great way for you to clear up any misunderstandings that you may have about an answer which you have already been given. When asking follow up questions, try to make them relevant to the last question that you asked and be sure to build on the previously obtained knowledge. Follow up questions not only help you to obtain the information which you are seeking, but they are also a great way to show the other individual that you are paying attention to their answers. Remember that when gathering quality information about a topic you might have to dig a little deeper!

Keep Questions Flowing in Order

Try to ask your questions in a logical order so that the other individual does not become confused. If you have to backtrack to previous questions or have to keep moving back and forth as the conversation proceeds, the other individual is likely to become confused or irritated which will likely make them less willing to put thought into the answers which they provide you with. Ensuring that your questions progress in a logical order will allow the other individual to guess which questions they may expect to come next. By being able to guess what questions come next, the other individual will feel more comfortable in talking to and sharing information with you. If the other individual is completely unable to guess what directions your questions are headed in they may feel like a trap or surprise is coming, and since people rarely like being cornered the person may become nervous and reserved.

Keep it Simple!

Asking specific questions is a great way to gain specific, useful information from the answers which you are given. Asking complicated or complex questions, however, can have much an opposite result. Sometimes the best way in which to gain the specific answers that you are seeking is to make sure that you are keeping your questions fairly simply. If you overcomplicate your questions or make them too complex, you run the risk of confusing the other individual by making it more difficult to not only understand your question but by also making it more difficult to answer your question at all. The other individual will likely not be impressed by the complexity of your question, and by making your question more complicated you may also be obscuring the true question that is being asked. As a general rule, if the other individual has to take more than a single moment to consider what your question means or how to interpret it, they are likely to misunderstand the question and answer it in such a way that may not be particularly useful to you in achieving your information goals. Remember to keep your questions simple so that there are no occurring misunderstandings!

Is Your Question Really a Question?

Asking questions that we already know the answers to is something that almost everyone is guilty of. You may think that it is beneficial to open a conversation with a question that you already know the answer to. However, this is usually not the case. When you ask a question that you already know the answer to, it is easy for the other person to guess that you know the answer and feel like you are trying to be sneaky or trick them. Starting a conversation in such a dishonest way is likely to be extremely counterproductive to your information goals. It is also very easy to allow your emotions or attitude to take over when asking a question which you already know, especially if the other individual does not answer the question exactly as you expect them to. When it comes to asking questions to another individual, be sure to keep in mind that you should avoid asking any questions which you already know the answer to. If you know the answer to a question already, the chances are that it will come out sounding more like an opinion or statement (whether you mean for it to or not). If you already know the answer but need this question to lead up to another question which you do not know the answer to, try changing the initial question to a statement instead. If you were meaning to ask the question "Did you call off last Wednesday?" just so that you could ask the follow-up question of "Why did you call off?", maybe you could just lead off with the statement "I know you called off last Wednesday" and then ask the question "Can you tell me why you called off?" Remember that if your question is not really a question, then it is more than likely just a waste of time and may be counterproductive to your information goals.

Choose Questions That Pull from Experience

When you are asking other individual questions to gather specific information from their answers, try to ask them questions that they will have to use their personal experience to answer. Questions that require someone to reflect on personal experience to answer have a higher tendency of being true and also more thoughtful. Anyone can easily recite knowledge that they have gained from a book or class to answer a question, though these answers may be relatively short or simple since it is just written memorization for the person answering the question. Questions that ask about another individual's experience, however, will most likely be answered in a thoughtful and detailed way (which may result in you receiving better answers to achieve your information goals). When another individual must reflect on previous experiences to answer a question, they are likely to feel as though you care about them in a more personal way or that you genuinely enjoy hearing about their past experiences. When a person enjoys sharing their experiences with you, they will be more willing to put time and thought into answering your questions so that you may more easily achieve your information goals.

Choose Questions That Provoke Thought

Some of the best and most effective questions that you can ask other people are those questions which provoke thought. Thought-provoking questions will get the other individual (whom you are questioning) thinking, making them more interested in the topic in question as well as the discussion which you are a part of (and asking questions in). You will receive better information and answers to your questions from someone who is interested in the conversation which they are a part of, that is why it is so important to begin with a few thought-provoking questions. When you are questioning another individual, you should aim to open up this individual's mind rather than asking questions that narrow the topic down to nothing. Thought-provoking questions may lead the other individual to consider other points that can improve the answer which they provide you with as well. If you ask a simple question, they will surely provide a simple answer. If you ask a thought-provoking question, however, they may provide you with that same answer but also offer a personal bit of experience or additional comment on their answer as well. Questions that cause an individual to take a moment to think about them are a wonderful way to add depth and substance to a conversation, and will surely add some "pizazz" to your list of previously prepared questions.

Ask Questions Logically

When you are asking an individual question to obtain specific information, it may be a good idea to lead off some of your questions with information that you already know. For example, news reporters often ask questions by leading off with previously obtained information first. A news reporter will usually phrase a question as "We know that ___________, so you can tell us how __________ will affect _________ in the future?" This proves the person whom you are questioning that you are educated on the topic in question and may make them more comfortable talking to you (the individual may provide you with better, more detailed answers if they are comfortable speaking with you). Asking questions logically is also a good tool for explaining your own thinking to the individual in question (this is especially useful if there is a part of the information that you do not fully understand). You may want to say something along the lines of "I already know __________, but how does that affect ___________ since _______________?" By explaining your thinking out loud, the individual in question will see that you have thoroughly considered this topic and have carefully chosen which questions to ask. Showing that you cared enough about this conversation ahead of time to prepare yourself will make the other individual respect you more and may want them to provide you with better information than if they were under the impression that you barely care about the topic which you were asking them to explain.

When you are sharing your previous knowledge about the topic with the individual in question, this may also be a good time to share any sources from which you have obtained your information. The chances are that if the individual knows enough about the topic in question to be providing you with new information that they are familiar with the other information sources which you may have come across. It is important to have confidence when asking some individual questions concerning a specific topic. Try not to be intimidated, do not allow yourself to come off as being shy. Show some confidence and be proud that you have put in the research necessary to ask intelligent/informed questions regarding this topic.

Chapter 3: Increase Your Emotional Intelligence

To build quality personal and professional relationships with others, you need to master two things: communication skills and emotional intelligence. This eBook is all about how to master communication skills so that you can effectively ask questions, solve problems, and communicate effectively. By effectively asking questions, you will be able to gather the much-needed information from the individuals who will be providing you with the answers to those questions. But what about emotional intelligence? Emotional intelligence can be defined as knowing and being able to evaluate emotions (yours and those of other people) so that you will be able to form better relationships and master communication with them. If you are going to be asking multiple questions to another person, it would be extremely helpful for you to first build some sort of relationship with them: this relationship could be personal or professional. Whatever the case may be, increasing your emotional intelligence is a great way for you to master the communication skills necessary to achieve your information goals. In this chapter, we have included several tips for you to increase your emotional intelligence which will help you to master overall communication skills.

One very helpful technique in developing or increasing emotional intelligence is to observe your personal thoughts and feelings. By observing your thoughts and feelings, you will better be able to control them so that you may use them to master your communication skills to ask questions effectively.

Empathy

Being empathetic means that you are open to or receptive to other people's feelings and emotions. Empathy is a great personal characteristic for an individual to possess as it allows the individual to be more intuitive when it comes to "reading" other people's thoughts, energies, and emotions. If you are questioning someone about a controversial topic or their personal experiences, empathy can be useful in helping you to remain considerate of their feelings and emotions so that they will still be willing to provide you with the answers which you are seeking. Individuals who are empathetic and display empathy are consistently known to be more "in tune" with their own feelings or emotions, which in turn also allows them to display higher levels of emotional intelligence than an individual who is without empathy. There are multiple ways for you to practice being more empathetic towards others. First, you can try to remember to always put your personal viewpoints and judgments aside so that you may try to see where the other person is coming from. Try to imagine being in their situation, and think about how you would feel if you were to find yourself in their position. Once you have imagined how you would feel in that situation, ask the other person how they plan to approach their problem and then take some time to think about how you would react in that situation. Would you handle it differently? Do you think you would react more or less emotionally if you were in that person's place? You can also be sure to take more time to listen to how other people feel rather than constantly offering your own input or advice. Before approaching someone else about a topic which may cause them to feel strong emotions, ask yourself how your questions may make them feel and determine if there is anything that you can do to minimalize any discomfort for the other person.

Question Yourself

One way to increase your emotional intelligence and improve your own relationships with others is to question your own various personal opinions. By reevaluating our thoughts and questioning our own opinions, we can better predict how other individuals may feel about and respond to our questions. By questioning our own opinions, we also offer ourselves the chance to consider what opinions may be held by others to increase our own understanding and empathy. Regardless of how you decide to go about it, questioning your own opinions is a great way to not only increase your emotional intelligence but will also result in you being more understanding and respectful of the different personal beliefs held by those around you. Remember that in questioning your personal opinions, no one is asking you to change your personal beliefs. Questioning your opinions is beneficial to you even if you hold the same beliefs at the end of each evaluation, as you have still gained the experience of considering other opinions and perspectives on the topic in question. Simply considering where other people may be gaining their beliefs from is a great way to practice being more open-minded and tolerant of your beliefs. Asking yourself your practice questions can offer you the chance to evaluate what sort of emotions these questions may cause within the other individual, and you can then evaluate what sort of answer they may give in response to this occurring emotion. Based on these predictions of the other person's emotions and response, you can then develop follow up questions to keep the conversation moving forward productively.

Intuition

Can you recall a time when you were asking someone a question and, though they said they were telling you the whole truth, you guessed that there was more to the story than what they were telling you? Sometimes our body's natural intuition can be a very valuable tool in asking effective questions and even thinking up essential follow up just "does not feel right" about the way in which they answered. Whether you are developing emotional intelligence, becoming better at problem-solving, or learning how to master various communication skills; listening to your body is key. Everyone has heard of the phrase "listening to your gut" or "gut-feeling," and both of these phrases refer to your body's ability to pick up on subtle cues that you may not notice and relay that information to you with no concrete evidence.

Your "gut-feeling" will present itself in a slightly different way each time that you experience it and is often different for everyone. Some of the most common physical cues that your body is intuitively picking up on subtle things around you are feelings of anxiety, "butterflies" in your abdomen, or feeling that the hairs on your arms or neck are standing upright. While there is no exact way to point out how your body's "gut-feeling" works, it all comes down to your brain's intuition. Your brain can pick up on very subtle changes or cues from the people and environment around you, changes that are so subtle that you may not notice them. Your brain, however, uses these subtle changes to help you to make good decisions or assessments about uncertain situations intuitively. Getting used to "following your gut" or giving credit to your intuitive brain may take some practice (and a lot of faith). However, this can really pay off in the end.

Learning to listen to your body and your mind's natural intuition will result in the development of an increased level of emotional intelligence, will allow you to make better decisions, and will also aid in your ability to figure out when additional questions need to be asked to gain the needed information. Try to remember that our bodies, and especially our brains, are very smart. Practice trusting in your mind's natural intuitions so that you may come to rely on it when you find that you have come to a "fork in the road" or are unsure with how to proceed in a given situation. If you find that you do not completely trust someone's answer to a given question, find a way to politely dig deeper to see if your body's natural intuition was correct all along!

Chapter 4: Quality Speaking

The way in which you ask questions determines the helpfulness of the answers that you will be met with, but did you know that asking quality questions is about more than just what questions you ask? Asking quality questions begins with the many characteristics that make up quality speaking skills. Everything from the words you use to the volume of your pitch will be heard and interpreted by the other person, and these characteristics will determine the way in which they respond to your questions. Improving your speaking skills is a great way to be sure that you are capable of asking effective questions that will help you to achieve your information goals.

Use Common Language

When you are entering a new conversation with another individual, especially a conversation in which you will be asking questions to gather specific information, it is important that you consider the experience of the other individual. Using appropriate language when asking questions can easily decide whether you obtain quality and helpful answers or not. If you know that the individual is more experienced about the topic in question than you are, it may be a good idea to become familiar with some more advanced terminology so that they do not become bored by more basic questions: if you bore the other individual, they may be more reluctant to put forth the thought and effort to giving you quality answers to your questions. Be sure to use language that is easy for both you and the other individual to understand. Using common language is important for when you are asking questions to the other individual so that they can provide you with complete and quality answers.

Speak with Confidence

Speaking with confidence is important whether you are asking questions, answering questions, or just having a casual conversation with one or multiple other individuals. Speaking with confidence will make the other party feel like you are truly interested in your topic and may make them more willing to answer any questions that you may have. To speak with confidence, you may want to try practicing your questions or key points of the conversation before you actually have to speak on the topic. People are more likely to take you seriously, pay attention, and value your input if you are speaking in a confident manner. Think of the last time you listened to someone speak who did not seem to be very confident in what they were saying. Did you take them seriously? Did you think they were very knowledgeable about their topic? Do any of these have to do with the amount of confidence that they displayed? The best way to speak with confidence is to know what you want to say to other people, thoroughly research the topic in discussion, and practice your key points well I ahead of time so that you are not lost or confused as you present your information.

Confidence effects ourselves and our habits in numerous ways, all of which are important in our ventures to mastering communication skills and speaking in a high-quality manner. Having confidence is vital in the way that we handle ourselves in stressful situations, and let's be honest, the road to success is not always going to be stress-free. Asking questions to someone who is reserved or unfriendly may cause stress, and sometimes just preparing for an upcoming interview or important conversation can prove to be stressful. Having confidence in one's self means that you will be more motivated to begin a project or tackle a challenge, two things that will be critical in mastering communication skills. Another way that confidence directly leads to your ability or inability to effectively ask questions is that a lack of confidence often leads to your wanting to hold back in various situations (and how can you ask effective questions if you are afraid to speak openly and honestly?). If you have a lack of self-confidence, you are more likely to be shy or to shy away from questions that you may feel uncomfortable asking or that you may feel you are too inexperienced on the topic to ask. These missed opportunities could potentially be the difference between whether you can achieve your information goals or not.

There have actually been studies done to prove that confidence is a key factor in one's ability to accomplish specific goals or achieve general success in life. An article written in The Atlantic quotes "Taking action bolsters one's belief in one's ability to succeed. So confidence accumulates--through hard work, through success, and even through failure." To gain confidence, you will be forced to try new things so that you can later Two quotes to consider relating to the importance of confidence both in personal and professional goals: "When it comes to confidence, one thing is certain: truly confident people always have the upper hand over the doubtful and the skittish, because they inspire others and they make things happen" (Travis Bradberry, Forbes) and "Whether you think you can, or you think you can't- you're right" (Henry Ford). Try to remember each of these quotes the next time you find yourself lacking confidence in achieving a goal or developing mental toughness.

Believing in yourself and having some level of self-confidence may actually be just as important to success as education, people skills, communication skills, or work experience. The way one carries themselves says a lot about a person, and whether you are asking specific questions to gather information or answering questions asked in response to your own; confidence is key! The next time you set a goal for yourself, do not think about what is at stake if you fail and do not think about what disappointment you may feel with that failure. Instead of focusing on what could go wrong or what would happen if you fail, focus your energy instead on further training and preparation that will help you succeed in achieving your goal. If you find yourself with the attitude that failure is a likely outcome of your effort, you may develop the "why bother?" attitude with it, which will definitely reduce your chances of succeeding in your personal or professional goals.

The possession of self-confidence is vital not only to developing communication skills but also to achieve any information goals which you have set for yourself. Marcus

Garvey is a Jamaican political leader who has been quoted as saying "If you have no confidence in self, you are twice defeated in the race of life." Garvey's quote illustrates the importance of maintaining self-confidence to achieve both short and long-term goals. Some individuals are fairly self-confident by nature, but for other's the development of self-confidence will take some time and coaching.

Speak Slowly & Precise

A great way to be sure that you understand others is to develop effective communication skills. More often than not, misunderstandings between ourselves and other individuals are the result of simple miscommunication problems. You will no doubt have a much easier time understanding the viewpoints and opinions of others if you can effectively communicate with them. Be sure to ask direct questions and give honest/complete answers when having a conversation, this will eliminate many possible misunderstandings from arising. It is also important to remember that when you are having a conversation with someone, you must try to maintain pleasant eye contact and ask questions when needed. If you are unsure of something that the other individual is telling you, speak up and ask questions! Many of us are afraid to ask questions (we may feel stupid or feel like we are interrupting), but it is better to ask questions now then to find out there was a huge misunderstanding later on. Clear communication also relies heavily on the messages you send out verbally to others and how they are sent. Make sure that you are speaking clearly (do not mumble) and that your speaking voice is loud enough to be heard without too much effort being required of the other individual. Lastly, (we can't stress this enough) if you are unsure of what you are being told please ask for clarification so that you may understand others better!

When you are asking another person questions, or even just having an informative conversation with another person, it is important that you speak at a rate of speed that is slow enough to be understood by any other people involved. If you are speaking too quickly, the other individual may not understand your questions which may make it very difficult for them to provide you with quality answers. To be sure that your questions are understood and answered completely, make sure that you are speaking slow enough for the other person to follow and understand what you are saying. Speaking slowly can be difficult when you are angry, in a hurry, or emotional about the topic in discussion. Whatever the case may be, make sure that you keep your rate of speed for speaking in mind so that you are always fully understood. Precision is also an important factor to consider when asking other individual questions. Make sure that you are pronouncing your words clearly and precisely so that you are not mumbling. A poor pronunciation of your words can quickly lead to a misunderstanding between yourself and other individuals, which can greatly inhibit your chances for gathering quality answers to your questions.

Breathe

When you are asking someone important questions about a topic, it may be easy to overlook your breathing practices. If you go into a conversation that is causing you to be nervous or anxious, your breathing may become shallow or rapid. If your breathing is quickened, you may find yourself having trouble finishing longer sentences or thoughts without having to take in another quick, sharp breath. If your breathing becomes too rapid, however, your brain will not be able to obtain an adequate amount of oxygen which may cause you to become dizzy or have a headache. Breathing is perhaps the most natural thing that our bodies know how to do. However, it is something that we may forget to fully take advantage of in stressful situations. When we are nervous or stressed our breathing might become rapid and shallow. Incorrect breathing can result in a feeling of anxiety or panic, which will not allow us to achieve our peak performance. Breathing as you make a presentation or even just present previously gained knowledge during a conversation make take practice, but it is a fairly easy skill to develop as well as maintain. Before you begin a presentation or lengthy conversation to gather information, take five deep breathes. Then, be sure to check your speaking speed periodically throughout your speech or conversations and make adjustments as needed.

Almost everyone has been in that same situation: you are overly stressed or emotional, and somebody says to you "just breathe." Why is it that some people think that simply breathing will help you to solve your problems? Well, because it can! Breathing may not show you what questions to ask, research the chosen topic, or ask the questions for you; but correct breathing offers your body numerous health benefits that will make it easier for you to remain calm and focused while delivering your questions to achieve your information goals. When you are feeling stressed, upset, or angry, it can be very difficult to focus on being productive or optimific. Deep breathing exercises help you to reduce stress, release toxins from the body, strengthen abdominal muscles, and decrease blood pressure. By taking a minute (or five) when you are feeling stressed or overwhelmed, you allow your body the chance to process the events and find a logical solution that is beneficial to you. Consider it this way: when you are feeling emotional or overwhelmed, you may begin to practice a more rapid rate of breathing whether you intend to or not. Rapid, shallow breathing decreases the amount of oxygen your body is provided with: how can you expect your body (and especially your brain) to function without oxygen?

How to Practice Deep Breathing:

Practicing deep breathing is a lot like meditation, but you can practice your deep breathing exercises anywhere! No matter where you are (on the way to work, in a meeting, at the gym, or watching television at home) you can ground yourself and bring peace to your mind by taking a few moments to focus on deep breathing. To practice deep breathing, you should first make sure that you have good posture. Make sure that, whether you are sitting or standing, your back is straight and your shoulders are back. Once you have correct posture, inhale a single deep breathe over the course of three seconds. Hold this inhaled breath in for two seconds, and then slowly exhale the breath over the course of three seconds. Remember the rule whenever you want to practice your deep breathing exercises: 3-2-3. Repeat these three steps multiple times until you begin to feel your mind slow down, your heart rate decrease, and your body relax. Once your thoughts have stopped racing, and your body is more relaxed, you will be able to tackle any challenge and overcome any problems set before you.

By practicing deep breathing exercises, you will be able to make sure that you are well relaxed and prepared to conquer the battle ahead: okay, maybe not a battle but breathing can help you effectively ask questions in a relaxed and confident way!

Use Perfect Posture

Maintaining perfect posture has been shown to offer numerous health benefits, but did you know that maintaining good posture can also help to improve your speaking abilities greatly. Having good posture can result in an increase in your confidence which can gain you more respect as you present information or ask questions about your topic. You may also want to consider the way in which you present yourself when you are asking questions with the goal of gathering specific information, and posture plays a large role in your self-presentation. The way in which you carry yourself says a lot about you to the people with which you surround yourself. By maintaining correct posture, you are more likely to feel self-confident and perform better. Using a job interview as an example again, maintaining correct posture is vitally important. Slouching and dragging your feet will not look good to the people whom you are trying to impress during your job interview and will likely not make you feel very confident about your qualifications either. Contrarily, if you sit up straight and present yourself well, you are more likely to breathe deeply, speak eloquently, and have an increased level of self-confidence that can result in better performance during the interview. The individual whom you are expecting to answer your questions will have a greater sense of respect for you if you display correct posture, rather than if you attempt to ask your questions while you are slumped over or leaning on a piece of nearby furniture. When asking your questions, stand up straight and try to keep your shoulders back!

Stay Hydrated

Staying hydrated may not directly benefit your ability to ask effective questions, but by staying hydrated, you will be able to avoid several problems that could greatly affect your question asking ability. If you allow yourself to become dehydrated you may experience dry mouth, and how can you possibly ask questions effectively if your mouth is as dry as the Sahara Desert? Making sure that your body is adequately hydrated can also greatly improve your mood, thus providing you with the positive motivation needed to ask the necessary questions to achieve your information goals. If you find yourself unable to concentrate or even possibly yawning as you attempt to gather vital information by asking questions about the topic at hand, drinking more water may be able to help to eliminate this problem in the future. Drinking increased amounts of water can also be beneficial in helping to fight fatigue, and you may be hard-pressed to find the ability to ask effective questions if your body is putting all of its energy into taking a nap. Before entering a conversation in which you are seeking information, try to drink a full bottle of water roughly an hour beforehand. This added hydration will help to prevent headaches, and muscle cramps that can be counterproductive to your information goals, drinking more water will also help you be able to maintain focus better as you ask your questions politely and confidently!

Control Pitch

When you are asking questions, it is important to remember to control your voice's pitch. Practice asking your specific questions ahead of time so that you can see how you sound. When it comes to asking questions, it is not always what you say, but more how you say it that determines the type of answer you will receive. Whether your pitch is high or low, pitch is the voice characteristic that most determines how your emotions are read when you speak to others. People can often tell what sort of mood you are in based on your pitch, so it is important to keep this in mind and pleasant as you are asking questions so that you do not inadvertently come off as being in a bad mood. It is also important to consider that your pitch should slightly fluctuate as you speak and ask questions: you do not want to make your questions sound boring by having your voice sound too flat or monotone.

Control Volume

While often overlooked, voice pitch and voice volume are key components to mastering effective communication skills. Not only is your voice's pitch an important component in effectively asking questions, but equally important to pitch is your voice's volume. If you speak too quietly, you may not be heard and run the risk of your questions being ignored or misunderstood due to insufficient vocal volume. If you speak too loudly, you may come off as being offensive or arrogant which can result in your listener being less willing to answer your questions in a lengthy, detailed fashion or at all. If you are having trouble finding the correct volume to speak or ask questions with for your voice, it may be a confidence issue as well as a volume issue. If you are too confident you may find that your voice volume is much higher (louder) than you may have originally anticipated. Conversely, if you lack confidence in your questions, then you may find you are having trouble getting your voice volume loud enough to be respected and well understood. Try asking the questions to yourself or to a close friend for practice to make sure that you are putting adequate volume behind them to be understood. Emotions also have a lot to do with your voice's volume. If the conversation is turning into more of a debate, you may find yourself defending your key points and asking more pointed questions than you had originally planned. As a general rule, as your emotions rise so does your voice. Raising your voice at an individual whom you need to answer your questions to achieve your information goals is not going to be very helpful to you, so try to practice controlling your volume regardless of how you are feeling at the time of a conversation. Being able to control your voice's volume in every scenario will ensure that your questions are always heard, understood, and respected.

Chapter 5: Be Courteous and Polite

Do Not Interrupt

When you are asking someone multiple questions to gather information, you can certainly expect for a conversation to develop and take place. As the person, you are questioning tries their best to answer your questions, make sure that you refrain from interrupting them. If you interrupt someone as they are answering your question (even if it is just to ask another question), they may not be able to answer the first question completely which can result in them leaving out crucial details that can help you to achieve your information goals. Interrupting someone mid-sentence is also extremely disrespectful, and disrespecting someone is a sure-fire way to miss out on essential information as they will be much less willing to answer you if they feel disrespected. Be sure that you always allow someone adequate time to answer a question before making a comment or moving on to the next question. Even if you are sure that they have already finished answering your question, allow an extra two or three seconds to pass before moving on so that they do not feel cut off or rushed. If you are anything like most people, you hate being interrupted while having a conversation with someone else. One of the most basic courtesies that you can try to adhere to when asking questions is affording others the same kindness that you would like to experience in not being interrupted as you are speaking.

Always Be Polite

Not interrupting others as they are answering your questions is a good way to make sure that you are politely asking questions to others. However, there are other ways to be sure you are using your manners when taking part in a conversation as well. When asking questions to others, it is also essential to try to keep a neutral attitude so that the other party feels their opinion is respected. Keeping a neutral attitude when asking questions can be difficult, especially if the topic in question is a controversial topic such as abortion or gun control. However, if you feel strongly about the topic in question and that shows in your questioning the other individual may not feel comfortable answering your questions honestly if their views differ from your own. By wording your questions from a neutral point of view, you will be much more likely to gain honest and unbiased answers from the other individual. Remaining neutral in a conversation will also ensure that you do not offend the other individual. If someone offended you and then proceeded to ask you for information on a given topic, would you be willing to give them an honest and unbiased answer? Would you be able to answer without allowing your emotions to speak for you? After someone offended you, would you think that they deserve the time required to give them an informed and thoughtful response? Consider these things as you word your questions for an upcoming conversation, especially if the topic is the least bit controversial. Remembering your manners can be extremely helpful in asking effective questions and gaining necessary information for your information goals.

It's Not About You

When asking questions about a specific topic to another individual, try to keep the conversation directed away from yourself. Avoid getting caught up in having "story time" or sharing personal experiences as these can be very time-consuming and quickly lead to you getting distracted by other thoughts or ideas. If the conversation containing essential information getting questions overtaken by personal stories, you may miss some vital answers to your questions. Allowing the conversation to be centered on you can be very counterproductive to your information goals.

Speaking about yourself the whole time can make the conversation boring and uninteresting for the other individual. It's like hosting a talk show but not letting the guests talk.

Ask for Permission

When you are asking questions for the sole purpose of gathering information about a specific topic, it is usually a good idea to begin by asking permission. Once you begin asking questions the other person will likely be able to figure out what type of information you are interested in and what your information goals may be, so it is considered polite for you to begin by asking if you have permission to ask the person several questions about the given topic. Before beginning with your questions, be sure to start with something along the lines of "Would it be okay if I ask you a few questions about____________?" or "Would you mind answering a few questions that I have about

_______________?”. The other individual is likely to appreciate that you were considerate enough to ask for permission to question them before you began which may result in them being more willing to answer your questions thoughtfully and honestly.

Chapter 6: Be Specific

General questions will often lead to the reception of general answers, which may be fine to start. However, to achieve your information goals, you will likely need to gather much more specific information. When you begin asking your practiced and prepared questions, you may want to start with a general question to lead to the more specific ones. Asking general questions just as an opener can help to break the ice and to open a comfortable conversation between you and the individual in question. While general questions are great conversation starters, it is important to achieving your information goals that you focus the bulk of the questions on obtaining very specific answers and information.

Specific Wording

We have already discussed how counterproductive misunderstandings can be when it comes to achieving your information goals, and one of the best ways to avoid misunderstandings is to be sure that your questions are always as specific as possible. For the other person to answer your questions completely and thoughtfully, it is vital that they fully understand what you are asking. If you ask questions that are too general in nature, you may receive answers that are also general in nature, and these may not be extremely helpful in achieving your information goals. To gain useful and specific information, be sure to ask questions that are not able to be misinterpreted. Make sure to use specific key terms, dates, and names when necessary to gain the need information. If you are not sure if your questions are worded in too general a manner, try asking yourself them for practice first. What sort of answer are you hoping for from this question? Does the question use specific or general wording? Does the way in which the question is worded prompt you for a detailed answer or a short, general answer? Consider each of these questions as a way to determine how to word your questions so that you can be sure to receive the best possible answers.

Make Your Goals Known

Another great way to be sure that your questions contain specific wording so that they are met with detailed answers is to make your information goals known to the individual in question. If the other individual is under the assumption that you are just asking these questions out of curiosity, they may feel that you will do better research on your own later on, so they do not need to provide such thoughtful answers. However, if you make your goals known to the person in question they may be more willing to put both more time and thought into their answers to help you to achieve those goals. For example, you can explain that you are writing an article about __________ or hoping to learn more about __________ before you begin asking questions. Making your goals for the questions known can also help the other individual to feel that you are really interested in and committed to learning about this topic, which can only help to increase their willingness to help you by answering your questions.

Chapter 7: Prepare for Discussion

When you are asking multiple questions to another individual to gather information about a specific topic, it is important that you prepare yourself for the almost inevitability that a discussion will develop. Whether the other person simply answers your questions or offers additional comments, it is important that you expect and be able to correctly handle a developing conversation that has stemmed from your questions.

Open a Conversation

To prepare for a conversation, it can help if you are the one who opens it, to begin with. If you are looking to ask an individual specific questions to gather information, they may be more willing to offer you answers if you are friendly enough to open a conversation with them about the general topic. Consider which situation is more friendly and comfortable: answering only specific questions without any background, or answering questions as part of a bigger, more general conversation. Asking multiple specific questions to an individual can begin to feel more like an interview or interrogation if not done correctly, which is why you can comfortably lay the groundwork for these questions by opening a discussion with the other individual ahead of time.

Be Prepared for Discussion

Before opening a conversation or asking questions to the other person, you should always make sure that you are prepared for a discussion to develop. In preparing for a discussion to develop after you have asked multiple questions, try to make sure that you have thoroughly researched your topic so that you can answer any questions that the other person may have for you in return. It is also a good idea, in preparing for a discussion, to try to put yourself in the other person's shoes so that you may anticipate some of the questions or comments which they might have for you. Make sure that you have the information necessary to keep these conversations going if you are unable to take part in an educated discussion the other individual will be less likely to consider or respect your point of view of the topic in question. Preparing for a discussion may seem like a waste of time or a meaningless practice, but there is nothing worse than being in the middle of a conversation and only then finding out how unprepared you truly are. If you are wondering if discussion preparation is really necessary for effectively asking questions just remember Benjamin Franklin's quote "By failing to prepare, you are preparing to fail"!

Show Appreciation for Answers/Feedback

When you are asking questions to other people, they are inevitably going to have feedback, answers, and possibly more questions for you. Whether their answers or feedback or something that you agree with or not, it is important that you show appreciation for these answers regardless. People who know that you do not appreciate their input are going to be hesitant to answer any of your questions in the future regardless of the topic of interest. Always make sure that you thank the other person for answering your questions and also thank them for offering any additional input or comments on the topic. Showing appreciation for another individual's help could make them much more willing to help you or answer any additional questions in the future. If you seem ungrateful for a person's help or you allow yourself to show obvious disagreement about their answers or comments you may find yourself running out of people to ask your questions to in the future. Showing appreciation for the answers, you are given to your questions obviously ties into your ability to remain polite in asking questions as well as your ability to prepare for a discussion properly. Learning how to use criticism constructively is essential to minimalizing the amount of stress that impacts your body's health and happiness. Criticism and feedback (when used in a positive, constructive manner) can be used to get to know more about yourself (your strengths and weaknesses) as well as to build stronger relationships with those around you.

Reception: It is important for you to always remain open to criticism and feedback so that you may later use them to better yourself and your future experiences. If you are not receptive to feedback, you are not allowing yourself the opportunity to use the objective opinions of others as a tool. For many people, listening to criticism is hard. Hearing feedback and criticism from those around you can be made even harder if the person offering their opinion is not particularly good at communicating or is too blunt in expressing themselves. Whatever the case, it is important for you to try to remain "thick skinned" so that you can use this feedback constructively rather than being offended by it. Be sure to use criticism as a tool to succeed in the future rather than allowing it to become another obstacle in your path to success. When receiving negative feedback or criticism, your body's natural response may be to become defensive or find an excuse for your actions. When receiving criticism, try your best to stop your body's initial reaction. Take time to listen to the feedback entirely before allowing yourself to react, then evaluate the given feedback to determine if there was any validity to it. Be sure to thank the person for their input and opinions, and if possible ask if you may follow up on that criticism after a set time period (usually two or three weeks) to see if the individual has noticed any significant improvement. You may, of course, ask questions while receiving feedback though it is vital that you remain objective and do not allow yourself to become defensive. Lastly, always remember the multiple benefits of receiving this feedback from other individuals. When receiving feedback, be sure to continuously remind yourself that criticism is a good thing and can even be used to your advantage as a wonderful tool for success. Once you have conditioned yourself to be open to feedback and criticism, you can then use this feedback to achieve success in your future goals.

<u>*Utilization:*</u> The first step to using feedback to your advantage (as a way to develop better relationships and be more successful in achieving your goals) is, of course, to be sure that you are open to the reception of criticism. After conditioning yourself to receive criticism without having an immediate reaction, you can then use this criticism as a vital tool. When it comes to the utilization of feedback in the form of constructive criticism, the first step is to log and store this feedback so that it may be referenced at a later date (as needed). While the comments given may be fresh in your mind immediately after receiving feedback, this will likely not be the case in a few weeks or months. If you journal the oral feedback upon reception or store papers on which written feedback was given, you will be able to access this feedback at a later date to ensure that you have made some progress with it, or you will be able to use it to focus on another area that was mentioned during the initial critiquing. When utilizing feedback, it is also important to remember to focus on a single area at a time. Choose a specific area upon which you received constructive criticism, and focus on improving this area before moving on to the next. If you are attempting to better yourself overall, you are likely to be less successful than if you set a single, specific goal for yourself. It is easier to achieve a single, small goal than it is to achieve a broader goal.

<u>*One last thing:*</u> regardless of whether the feedback you have been given is mostly positive or negative, always try to respond in a kind and respectful manner. If you have been given negative feedback, it may be difficult to respond in a kind way immediately. However, this will really pay off in the future. If you snap at the individual who is giving you feedback (or become defensive and emotional), they may be hesitant to offer any feedback or advice in the future (which may be counterproductive to your long-term goals). When given feedback or constructive criticism always follow these simple steps: (1) Say "Thank You" and mean it. Whether the feedback is good or bad, it can still be used as a valuable tool to succeed in the future. (2) Smile! Smiling may be hard to do when you've just been given negative feedback, but it will make you appear less bothered by the constructive criticism and can actually help you to feel better immediately.

Avoid Yes or No Questions

When you are asking questions about your chosen topic to another individual try to always avoid yes or no questions. Yes or no questions can make the other person feel as though you have not put in adequate effort to developing these questions, making them more likely to put less thought and effort into answering them. Open-ended questions are much more preferable to yes or no questions as they will force the other individual to answer more thoughtfully, including more detail and information in their answers than a simple yes or no would provide you with. By asking only yes or no questions, you may also find that you are being given incomplete information as part of the answers you receive. To obtain only factual and complete information always make sure to ask specific open-ended questions. Having trouble thinking of good open-ended questions? Try to ask questions starting with the words would who how when where or why. These words will lead the other individual into putting more thought into their answers which will result in you being one step closer to achieving your information goals.

Silence and Suspense

We have already discussed how waiting a few extra seconds after being provided with an answer will ensure that you do not interrupt the other person, but allowing time to pass after asking a question and receiving an answer may result in you receiving additional information as well. We have all seen the familiar scene in movies or television shows: the law enforcement officer is interrogating a suspect and rather than continuously asking questions, they just stare at the suspect in silence until they crack and tell them everything! This tactic will not be nearly as dramatic when you use it to ask other people questions, but it can help you to gain additional information just the same. People often become uncomfortable with silence, and more often than not they feel the need to fill the silence by talking. If you ask a question and the pause, or receive an answer and then pause, you may find that the individual being questioned is more willing to offer additional information to their answer to shorten the silence. For this tactic to work, you need to make sure that you can be comfortable enduring silent periods first. Remember that detectives and law enforcement officials often use silence to gain additional information about their questions because people become uncomfortable with silence.

Conclusion

Thank you again for purchasing this book, *"How to Ask Questions: The Right Way"*.

I hope this book was able to help you to learn how to master the communication skills necessary to ask questions thoughtfully and effectively. The ability to ask questions effectively is a skill that everyone should possess, as questions are vital communication tools in numerous situations and life events. Asking questions is not only a great way to gain additional information when needed, but asking questions can also help you to initiate conversations with other individuals. Yes, asking questions can make you wiser and more social.

The next step is to utilize the information contained in this book so that you can be sure that you ask the necessary questions needed to gather important information from other people.

Things may not be very easy for you in the beginning – especially if you are someone who's always reserved. But, as you continue to apply the techniques in this book, you will find soon that you have the confidence to ask questions. When asking questions, prepare yourself to making a discussion with someone.

Thank you and good luck!

HOW TO
BE FUNNY
THE RIGHT WAY
The Only 7 Steps You Need to Master Comedy,
Conversational Humor and Making People Laugh Today
DEAN MACK

BOOK 3: HOW TO BE FUNNY

THE RIGHT WAY

The Only 7 Steps You Need to Master Comedy, Conversational Humor and Making People Laugh Today

Dean Mack

Respective authors own all copyrights not held by the publisher.

The information herein is offered for informational purposes solely, and is universal as so. The presentation of the information is without contract or any type of guarantee assurance.

The trademarks that are used are without any consent, and the publication of the trademark is without permission or backing by the trademark owner. All trademarks and brands within this book are for clarifying purposes only and are the owned by the owners themselves, not affiliated with this document.

Table of Contents

Introduction

Thank you and congratulations for purchasing *"How to Be Funny: The Right Way"*.

This book was designed to help you master the art of humor. Humor has been said to help people in many ways. Not only does it make you more approachable and personable for people you communicate with, but it can actually have many benefits for yourself as well. Having a strong sense of humor has been known to help people cope with physical and mental challenges that they may face in life, such as stress or other ailments. It helps bring light to otherwise difficult situations and can increase the positive experiences shared between yourself and others. Laughing, which is often as a result of humor, is also known to have many positive benefits for people's health.

Having a strong sense of humor can benefit you in many powerful ways. For some, however, being funny does not come easily or naturally. If you find that you struggle to be funny, perhaps because you tend to take things too seriously or you simply can't bring yourself to do it, this book will help you overcome that. These seven steps will help you identify how you can become funnier, and teach you the way to achieve that in your life. As a result, you will be able to derive all of the social and personal benefits that come from being a funnier person. If you are ready for all of these benefits, read on! And please, enjoy!

Chapter 1: The Importance of Humor

Although this book is about learning to be funnier, why don't we take a moment to understand why a sense of humor is so important for us? Sometimes, a great way to help yourself come out of your shell is to understand how powerful humor can be. When you realize what a positive impact it can have on your life and the life of others, it can be easier for you to stop viewing comedy and humor from a negative and fearful standpoint and start viewing it as a positive and healthy trait.

Funny People Are More Likeable

People love being in a good mood and feeling positive about themselves and their life. Laughing as a result of someone being funny is a great way to get in a good mood. Therefore, if you are a funny person, you are much more likely to be liked by the people around you. When you make people laugh and make them feel happy, you are much easier for them to be around which makes you far more likable than someone who struggles to understand humor and is intense or overly serious all of the time.

Funny People Are Detail-Oriented

Believe it or not, people who are funny tend to be more focused on the details. Think of it this way, making a really good joke is not easy. The best ones are spontaneous, meaning you cannot come up with them in advance. There is no opportunity to prepare, you are simply given a moment, and you take it. This means that if you tend to be a funnier person, you are likely great at paying attention to details.

Studies have shown that some of the funniest jokes that people tell are focused on very minor details or a very specific part of a phrase that someone says. This means that someone who is generally considered funny can not only identify that particular detail or phrase, but they can also quickly come up with a witty or otherwise humorous response to it. As a result, they are both more detail-oriented and quicker thinkers.

Comedy and Humor Sets the Foundation for Bonding

As we have already discussed, funny people make people happy. People laugh, they are in a lighter and better mood, and they feel more positive when funny people are present. This also opens them up and sets the tone for bonding. When you can laugh as a result of someone says, you tend to automatically feel as though this person understands you on some deeper level. This feeling of someone relating to and understanding you is something that often helps most people feel closer to someone else. Therefore, when you are funny, you make it far easier for people to bond with you.

A great way to use this to your advantage is in business. If you are looking to close a business deal, start by opening with a quick little joke that everyone will understand. When people feel closer to you like this, they are far more likely to want to agree with you and do business with you. It can have a highly positive impact on your success in business. It can also help you be more successful with making friends, with fitting in to new situations, and with finding alliances in new places.

Funny People Are Always Invited

One fun little benefit of being the funny person is that funny people are nearly always invited to all functions. Because they are funny, know how to lighten the mood, and are likable, people want them around more. This means they are more likely to be invited to parties, social gatherings, and other events that are taking place. Funny people are the life of the party. They often get everyone relaxed and in a good mood, spread the positive vibes, and make things feel more comfortable and enjoyable. People want them around because they are great at making their gathering or event more enjoyable for their attendees, therefore making it a greater success.

This is a major benefit when it comes to business, especially. A good sense of humor is a great networking tool. By getting yourself invited to places, you can easily use your humor to bond with people and increase your network. If you are really good at it, you will leave a lasting impression, and people will be excited to call on you for their business needs.

People are More Productive When Humor is Involved

Stress is one of the biggest productivity killers. Stress can be caused in many ways, too. Feeling uncomfortable, pressured, out of place, or otherwise at odds with a task you are faced with can be stressful. This means that you are far less likely to get as much done, meaning you are not as productive. Having a light-hearted sense of humor can boost your mood, as well as the moods of those around you. As a result, everyone is likely to feel much less stressed, and therefore they will be more productive. Because they are lighter spirits, it is easier for them to stay focused, feel accomplished right from the start, and work tirelessly with a can-do attitude. If you want yourself or your team to be more productive, try increasing your sense of humor and bringing it to work with you.

People are More Trusting of Funny People

When someone can make you laugh and make you feel as though they understand you, you are much more likely to trust them. Therefore, if you are capable of making other people laugh, they are more likely to trust you. If you want to establish trust with people, such as new friends, business associates, or even people you are negotiating with, try using a sense of humor. Warm them up, make them feel connected to you, and use humor to set the grounds for trust. Not only will this make people trust you more, but it will also speed up the relationship-building process. This can make natural friendships bloom faster, and can make business dealings come to fruition quicker as well.

Humor Relieves Stress and Boosts Creativity

In addition to making people more productive, relieving stress also makes people more creative. Since your sense of humor is a great tool to use when you are trying to relieve people of stress, you can also call on it when you want people to be more creative! Call on your sense of humor, crack jokes, and lighten the mood. When you have, watch how everyone's attitudes transform, and they are more open, receptive, and creative about the task at hand. You can use this in your friends' circle, or even with business associates or employees to increase what they bring to the table at work. Humor is a fast and easy way to reduce stress, so don't be afraid to use this tool to your advantage!

Chapter 2: Take Risks

Many people struggle to be funny because they are afraid of taking risks. In humor, taking risks is the best opportunity to discover jokes that are actually funny. This technique gives you the opportunity to learn more about what types of jokes are well-received, and what kinds aren't. If you ever pay attention to any major comedians, you will notice that they are often big risk takers when they are telling jokes. This is how they can find new content, reach new heights in their comedy, and create brand new and incredible jokes that have not been already told by other people.

The first step to taking risks when you are learning to be funny is to start by lowering your expectations. A large reason why people are afraid of taking risks is that they don't want to be misunderstood or judged for the joke they have told. By keeping the joke to themselves rather than sharing it, they protect themselves from potential "rejection" that they may face from their peers for sharing a joke that may not be well-received. This may protect them, but it also stops them from being considered funny.

Lowering your expectations means sharing jokes regardless of what the potential outcome may be. When we tell jokes, especially when we are taking risks with our humor, there is always a strong chance that the joke won't work out. It may not be understood, or some people may not know how to interpret it without slightly judging you for the content. In fact, some people may judge you a lot based on what you have recently said. If you share your humorous jokes without the need for everyone to laugh for you to feel successful, it becomes a lot easier to share it without concern for how people receive it.

Now, there are some limitations when it comes to taking risks with comedy. Many people think that there aren't, but there truly are. The limitations are often based on your environment, the people you are communicating with, and other people in general. For example, you would not want to be sharing humorous jokes that played on racial stereotypes in an environment such as your work, or another professional environment. You also would never want to share overly racist or sexist jokes that could have an underlying air of meanness to them. Although some of the best jokes are arguably the crude ones that step outside of the box of common societal standards, you never want these jokes to get you into trouble. You also don't want to hurt the people you are communicating with. If you choose to use this type of humor, then refrain from sharing it openly with just anyone. Instead, share it with the people who would understand you and already know about your existing beliefs so that they can tell you are being funny and that you are not actually trying to be harmful to any particular group of people. Otherwise, leave it to the professional comedians who build their entire persona off of their jokes.

Another element to this statute of limitations around taking risks is your environment. If you are in a professional environment, you always want to air on the side of caution and avoid using jokes that are overly risqué. You don't want to be saying anything that could be taken wrong or could compromise your integrity with the company. Even if you think someone would understand the joke, be careful. You want to make sure that you are mindful of everyone in the surrounding area and how they may interpret the joke before sharing it if it comes to something such as your livelihood on the line. Instead of sharing risqué jokes at work, look to share ones that are more innocent and dry. Take risks in different ways, such as by going out on a limb to put a pun together or put an innocent play on words. Even if you don't get a lot of laughs, people will still likely consider you to be funny.

Aside from the limitations around being risky, it is important to understand the different types of results you may get from being risky with your humor. As you have already learned, the biggest reason people aren't riskier is that they don't want to be misunderstood, judged, or rejected as a result of their humorous attempts. While this may very well happen, it is often unlikely unless you are telling inappropriate jokes that are rude or otherwise offensive to the people around you. Just because you may not be the type of person to get easily offended does not mean that the people you are communicating with are the same way.

Other potential outcomes include: people smile at your joke, people laugh at your joke, or people share your joke with others and spread the joy around. Now, understand that not all jokes have the same effect on people. Just because someone only smiles or finds the joke clever doesn't mean they don't like it. Instead, it simply means the joke wasn't "ha-ha" funny to them. Alternatively, they may snicker or even full out laugh at your jokes. Finally, if they really like it, they may even adopt the joke themselves and share it with people they know. Consider all of these good outcomes as they all mean that the person you have shared the joke with enjoyed your sense of humor.

There is a saying that goes: "There is no such thing as a bad joke." This saying implies that you should never hold back a joke for fear of rejection. Instead, share every joke that comes to you. By doing this, you ensure that you never limit yourself from having great success with sharing a joke. You cannot be considered funny if you never take a crack at actually being funny, so don't hold back unless your joke is absolutely and completely inappropriate for the present situation.

Chapter 3: Study Comedies

This may seem a little intense for learning to be funny, but studying comedies is a great way to learn how to increase your sense of humor and have a greater ability to be funny. Comedians literally make a living off of being funny, so you can assume that they know a thing or two about it. By studying comedies, you give yourself the opportunity to see how the professional comedians make their jokes and what is so funny about them. You can also learn what type of comedy you like and what type you aren't so keen on.

When you are studying comedies, here are some things you can pay attention to:

The Jokes Themselves

Obviously, you want to pay attention to the actual jokes being told by the comedian. Take the time to understand why the jokes are funny, how they are structured, and what content is within the jokes. Jokes are funny for different reasons, and they are funny on different levels. As well, there are short one-liners and longer story-style jokes. Understanding each type and how they work is a good way to discover how you can use these in your own life.

Pay attention to how the comedian changes the jokes, too. They don't typically stand on stage and blurt out several one-liners over and over. Instead, the entire set is usually built in some form of story-line that they have created based on the jokes they have. Each unique joke will be a different length and contribute more information to the overall story. While you are not likely to be on set and sharing story-line jokes such as the comedians are, it will give you an idea of how you can flow between different lengths and connect them together in a conversation. For example, you may learn how you can use a story-style joke in the beginning and then later in the conversation add in a one-liner that elaborates on the joke you told previously. Using different lengths of your jokes is a good way to stop yourself from becoming predictive and potentially even annoying from either always using short one-liners or going into elaborate jokes every time.

Of course, you always want to pay attention to the content of the jokes, too. Learn to discover what content you like, what content is openly accepted by people, and which audiences prefer which type of content. Understanding these different levels of content will help you when it comes to timing your jokes. It will also help you discover your own style of humor, as we all tend to have slightly varying styles. Choosing one that is unique to you will not only make you funny, but it will also help you stand apart from other people with your unique sense of humor.

Body Language

Body language accounts for a large portion of our ability to communicate effectively with other people. Using our body language, we can convey what mood we are in and what our intentions are around what we are saying out loud. Naturally, comedians use body language when conveying their jokes. Studying the body language that they use is a great way to learn how they use their movements to truly convey what they are trying to say.

When you are studying the body language of comedians, you will notice that there are two types of comedians: those who use elaborate body language and move around a lot for their jokes and those who use smaller and more intentional gestures. Those who are elaborate tend to take up a lot of space on the stage, use props, and sometimes even act out parts of the joke to really increase the humorous level to it all. Those who move around less generally use small but very intentional movements that drive the point home.

Pay attention to how each of these unique body language styles contributes to the jokes themselves, as well as how it makes the comedian look. For some, the elaborated gestures make the jokes far funnier and more enjoyable. If you are in a situation where this is acceptable, such as a party or another form of casual social gathering, you may choose to use elaborated gestures in your own humor as well. If you do, pay attention to how they use these gestures. In many instances, these gestures seem to have no limit. Many comedians will even get on the floor and flop around if it means that they can increase the humor in their joke. Practice using more elaborated and grand gestures in your own jokes so that you can get the hang of it and make use of it when the occasion permits.

You also want to pay attention to how the smaller gestures are used. When it comes to conversational humor, these tend to be more commonly accepted. For example, at work, you likely don't want to be flopping around on the floor to contribute to the humorous element of your joke. So, learning to use these smaller and more intentional gestures is a great way for you to learn how you can use your body to increase your humor level in various situations where you need to be more presentable and calmer for the occasion.

Both forms of body language contribute greatly to the levels of humor that can be conveyed by you, the joke-teller. Understanding how they work, when they are each acceptable, and how you can make use of them with your own jokes is important to increasing how funny you are.

Tone of Voice

In addition to using body language to convey ourselves to other people, we also use our tone of voice. Naturally, your tone of voice when you are being funny is far different from your tone of voice when you are being serious. Unless, of course, you are using sarcasm. Then, you may keep your tone of voice completely serious and let the joke speak for itself. Even in that circumstance, however, you are still using your tone of voice to contribute to your joke.

To learn how the tone of voice can help you with your sense of humor, study how comedians use their voices. They often throw them, raise or lower their pitches, or even make use of funny accents or voices to get their jokes across. Pay attention to how they use each of these unique tones to make their good jokes great jokes. Notice when they raise their voice, when they lower it, and how the different tones all contribute to how funny a joke is.

When we are joking, keeping a monotonous voice is a good way to take away from the experience of your joke. People may get lost in how boring your voice sounds and not realize that you are, in fact, trying to be funny. Instead of having your impact lost due to a lack of understanding of how your voice plays into it, study and practice this part.

One good exercise to use when you are studying how the tone of voice works with jokes is to say the same joke in many different tones. Say it in a serious tone, in a happy tone, in a humorous tone, in a questioning tone, and even in an angry tone. The more tones you try, the better. Each time you say it, notice how differently the joke comes across. For increased impact, record yourself on a voice recorder when you are saying the jokes. That way, you can easily understand how the tone of voice impacts the entire joke.

You will likely find that different jokes work better with different tones. Just because you are trying to be funny does not mean that you need to be using a humorous tone. Instead, some jokes may be even funnier if you use an alternative emotion in your tone of voice. Pay attention to the different emotions comedians put behind different jokes and notice what it does for the joke itself. Then, try practicing that in your own life, with your own jokes!

The Comedian's Perspective on Themselves

Every good comedian can maintain a sense of humor, even when talking about themselves. During their skits, you will often see them making fun of themselves and playfully joking about themselves. One of the reasons this is so important is because it helps keep the perspective of the comedian light and gentle. Furthermore, it adds to the humor of the show.

Another reason why keeping a light-hearted sense of humor toward yourself is important is because it helps keep you from taking yourself too seriously. If you will recall, in Chapter 1 we talked about eliminating the expectations on what you want the outcome from your jokes to be like. One great way that you can remove these expectations *and* the fear of rejection is to stop taking yourself so seriously. By regarding yourself in a light-hearted manner, such as by having a sense of humor about yourself, you make it much easier for you to maintain this light-hearted sense of humor toward yourself if and when other people take you too seriously, too. Remember, some people are not going to understand your jokes and others may even judge you for the jokes you choose to use. By intentionally taking away the pressure and refusing to take yourself too seriously, you make it much easier to stop yourself from worrying about if and when other people take you too seriously as well.

When you are studying this part, pay attention to how and when comedians use this part of their humor. Often, this part is used almost like a shield to "protect" themselves from their audience. For example, if they use a particularly risqué joke, they may poke fun at themselves to lighten the mood. This serves in two ways: first, by showing the audience that they shouldn't take the comedian too seriously surrounding the joke. Second, it allows the audience to get a small peek into how the comedian actually feels about that topic.

For example, say a comedian makes a joke about racial stereotypes. Perhaps she says:

"I'm such a typical white girl! Here I am with a pumpkin spiced latte in one hand, an iPhone in the other, and UGG boots on my feet. Heck, I even have one of those knitted white toques on with the pompom on the end. At this point..."

"... Just kidding, don't hate me, white girls. I love you, I really do. Especially because you make my comedy act just that much better."

Here, the comedian was able to tell a story and use racial stereotypes as an opportunity to heighten the humor in the joke. However, sometime after she got to the punchline and was closing the joke, she would say the second part. Here, she shows that she loves to make fun of white girl stereotypes, but also that she isn't actually prejudice towards white women. This means that if there *were* any easy-to-offend individuals in her audience, she gave them a quick insight into their actual opinion about white girl stereotypes.

This can go further, too. Some comedians will even talk in the third party, saying things like:

"I know what you're thinking right now. You're thinking, "Oh Kevin, you're such a jerk!" And you know what, yeah, I am a jerk. I know it, you know it. Let's move on now."

Here, Kevin poked fun at himself while staying light-hearted and also expressed his position to his audience.

One very important element of being able to be funny is knowing how to poke fun at yourself. People who cannot stay humorous toward themselves end up taking themselves too seriously. Then, because they do, they put far too much emphasis on the outcome of their jokes which, as you know, stirs up the fear around the entire subject of being funny in the first place.

Their Audience

When you are studying comedians, always take a moment to study who is in their audience as well. Most comedians have their own unique audience, which you often see through close-up shots during the filming of their acts. Paying attention to their audience gives you an idea of who their unique jokes appeal to most. Notice as much about the demographics as you can. Do they tend to be well-dressed business folk in an upscale setting? Are they everyday folk? Is there are particular culture or race that seems to be present more than any others? What age range is the audience?

Getting a clear idea of who is in the audience and comparing that to the jokes being told is a great way to get an insight as to what types of jokes appeal to which people. That way when you are in front of your own audience, whether it be a cashier or barista, or people in the lunchroom at work, you know what they are more inclined to laugh at. You can then tailor your jokes to suit your audience, which is something that most successful comedians are excellent at.

Whether You Personally Like It or Not

In addition to paying attention to the comedy act itself, pay attention to your own reactions toward it. What did you like about it? What did you not like about it? Understanding your own stance on various elements of the acts you watch is a great way to help you define your unique sense of humor. For example, do you tend to enjoy risqué jokes, or do you not like them? Are you more into dry humor, wordplay, or funny stories? What makes you enjoy the comedy most?

Building your unique sense of humor is important in helping you stand apart. You can do so by taking the elements of various comedians that you enjoy and putting them together to create your own unique sense of humor. For example, perhaps you like how Kevin Hart uses his tone of voice, but you prefer how Chelsea

Handler is more cool and sarcastic with her sense of humor. You know then that your own unique sense of humor should include cool sarcasm mixed with a touch of emotional tone to help create your own style.

Believe it or not, having your own style isn't only important if you want to be a comedian with a real audience. It also helps with virtually any type of humor you may want to use, including conversational humor and other more casual forms of humor. Moving away from generic forms of humor tends to make you even funnier because people aren't already used to the jokes you are using. Instead of using generic jokes they've likely heard, you will be more likely to say new things that keep them on their toes and prevent you from becoming predictable.

Chapter 4: Practice

As with any skill, practicing your ability to be funny is important. There are many ways that you can practice, including in everyday life and through intentional and planned practice sessions. Practicing being funny is the best way to build your sense of style, test your audience, discover what people like most, and generate new jokes that will keep people laughing when they listen to you. Let's explore some of the many opportunities you have to practice your sense of humor.

At Work

Naturally, one of the best places to practice your sense of humor is at work! Since you likely spend a great deal of time here, practicing your jokes on your coworkers is a great way to build your sense of humor. Not only that, but it will also lighten the mood at work and increase people's perceptions of you. They will no longer think of you as dry and potentially far too serious. Instead, they will think of you as witty and funny. This can improve the relationships you experience with coworkers and bosses, as long as you use your sense of humor properly.

Remember, at work you want to be more censored with your jokes. While taking risks is still valuable, you don't want to say anything that may be viewed as offensive to your audience. Especially in professional settings, you need to be more cautious of how you use your sense of humor. Try and use wordplay and jokes that are not based on sexism, racial stereotypes, or anything else with a potentially offensive or harmful nature. The only time when this limitation may be elevated is if you are in a private setting and you are around coworkers who are also your friends. Because you are closerto them, they will be clearer on the nature of your joke and will know whether or not you actually intend to be offensive. Since they already know you, they will be less likely to take personal offense to your joke, therefore eliminating any potential consequences you may face if you are not otherwise careful.

When at work, there are many opportunities to test your sense of humor. Try it out when you are chatting with people throughout the day. If a situation arises and you see the opportunity for a joke, such as when the printer experiences a paper jam or someone makes a mistake, take the opportunity and see what happens. The more you get to know how your co-workers respond to your sense of humor, the easier it will be to make jokes around them that they will genuinely enjoy.

On Friends and Family

Friends and family provide a great opportunity to take all limits off of your sense of humor and openly test out any jokes you may have. Because they know you so well and you know them so well, you are both on the same page when you make a joke. This is true no matter what the subject is. Of course, if you have a friend or family member who is particularly sensitive to a specific subject you may still want to avoid that subject around them to prevent your joke from being taken wrong. However, you can typically open up on the ones you are close with and share your sense of humor with them.

Look for opportunities during the conversation, when they make mistakes, or you make a mistake when you see something that is funny or strange, or at any other time that feels natural and authentic for the moment. If a joke comes to mind and you know the person you are with won't be upset or hurt by the joke, make it! Friends and family offer the best opportunity for you to test your jokes because they are less likely to harshly judge you for them. If you make a bad joke that truly is not funny after it has been said out loud, they are less likely to hold it against you or consider you to be "the weird guy in accounting" after you make it. Instead, they might joke about the joke you attempted, but they won't change or form their opinion on you based on your joke.

At Local Comedy Clubs

Local comedy clubs are a great opportunity to test out your sense of humor, especially if you are looking to gauge your abilities in front of an audience. Now, if you are the kind of person who is particularly fearful of audiences of and public speaking engagements, this may be harder for you. However, getting up in front of an audience and sharing your jokes with them is a great way to stop taking yourself so seriously and test your jokes out.

Local comedy clubs exist in almost every community, and they are a perfect chance for you to get up in front of an audience and have some fun. Even if you only do it once, it is a great experience. Plus, you might even find that you like it and want to do it again! If you find that you don't get the confidence to get up on stage, but you at least bring yourself to the club, you can also take it as an opportunity to learn about how other people enjoy humor and what types of jokes were successful and which weren't. In other words, you can have a night of entertainment while also studying comedy so that you can take your skills out into the world with you.

With Strangers You Meet

Every day you come across many people who are the perfect candidates for you to practice your sense of humor on! Baristas, cashiers, the people waiting in line with you, and in many other places. While it may not always be the perfect opportunity to practice your sense of humor, it doesn't mean you can't give it a try! If the opportunity does arise, don't be afraid to take it just because you don't know the person. Making a complete stranger laugh is a great way to boost your self-confidence and make telling jokes even easier in the future.

In Chance Encounters

Every single person is given random and chance encounters that are perfect for testing your humor on. For example, maybe you are at the grocery store, and you accidentally drop something when someone is next to you. This is a great opportunity to practice your sense of humor by playfully making fun of yourself and your mistake. You will likely come across many random opportunities such as this one where you can practice your sense of humor on the people around you. Don't pass up an opportunity just because you are nervous or you do not know the person next to you. Make it a fun experience that you both share together, even if you will never see each other again.

The more you practice building your sense of humor at every opportunity you get, the easier it will be for you to be funny. Not only will your self-confidence grow, but your knowledge around how to be funny in general will grow also. As a result of seeing people's expressions and how they respond to your jokes, how the joke made you feel, and what techniques you were able to use to make the joke even better, you will gain experience that will inevitably help you become much funnier overall.

Chapter 5: Know When to Be Funny

While you are in the process of mastering how to be funny, look for opportunities to learn more about timing your jokes. There are times when you should be funny and times when humor is not warranted for the situation. Knowing the difference between these circumstances and timing your jokes accordingly is a powerful way to ensure that you are appropriate for the occasion and that, when you do share them, your jokes are far more likely to be well-received.

There are three types of occasions you should know about when it comes to humor: those where humor is not warranted at all, those where light humor is acceptable, and those where you can be as funny as you desire to be. Let's take a look at each of these unique circumstances, including how you can tell what the mood calls for, jokes that are appropriate for each situation, and how the timing affects the quality of your joke.

When You Shouldn't Be Funny

When you are learning to be funny, one particular situation you need to be extremely mindful of is when *not* to be funny. While building a sense of humor is admirable, not every situation warrants humor. If you are funny when the mood does not call for it, there is a good chance that your humor will not be well-received. It may cause people to judge you, consider you to be incapable of being serious, or even consider you to be heartless or thoughtless. Humor is not meant to be something that makes people judge you or like you less. Therefore, you want to make sure that you are not using it at entirely inappropriate times. Here are some examples of when the mood would *not* call for humor:

- Serious work situations (e.g., having a sensitive conversation with your boss or employee, during serious business negotiations and meetings)
- Certain personal events (e.g., funerals)
- When someone is hurt (e.g., joking about divorce when someone is currently feeling the pain from their own divorce, *unless* you are close to that person and know for sure that they will appreciate the joke)
- As a shield against vulnerable situations (e.g., a romantic partner wants to discuss your future, and you use humor to avoid the topic)

Using humor at the wrong time can make you seem juvenile or incapable of taking things seriously. There are certain situations where people expect all parties involved to be serious and genuine. Using humor during these times can result in you making the situation uncomfortable and causing for people to become upset with you.

A good rule of thumb is that, if you are at all doubting how well-received your humor will be, because of the situation itself and *not* merely because of your own uncertainty or fear of embarrassment, avoid humor. While there are some instances where you may simply be afraid of the joke not being received, as we have previously discussed, there are many others where jokes would not be well-received because of the circumstances and not necessarily because it was a bad joke.

One of the most important parts of being funny is knowing *when* to be funny. Take care to work on practicing this particular skill when you are building your sense of humor. This will ensure that you build it properly and that your sense of humor does not become a fault.

When Light Humor is Acceptable

There are certain circumstances where light humor is acceptable, but full-blown humor is not. These circumstances vary and often depend on who is involved in the situation as opposed to the personthemselves. For example, say you get into a fender bender. If you are with someone such as a business associate you don't know well, making fun of the situation may not be ideal. However, if you are with a friend and no one is seriously injured, cracking a joke at someone's driving skills may be acceptable.

Determining whether light humor is acceptable or not can be done by knowing how close you are to the person or people you are surrounded by. If you are not very close to them *and* you doubt yourself, it is best to stay on the safe side and avoid making any jokes. If you are close to the person, however, and you know that they would understand your sense of humor, cracking light jokes at the situation is likely acceptable.

When it comes to light humor, avoid using anything too heavy. Jokes based on race, sex, and often even culturally-based jokes are often inappropriate in these circumstances. Again, use your best judgment based on the situation and who you are with. If you know them well enough that you know they will receive the joke properly, you are likely fine to go ahead and make it. If you don't, don't risk it.

When You Can Be as Funny as You Wish

Some situations have no limit on the amount of humor you can use. For these circumstances, you are not required to hold back because there is no reason to. There are typically no heavy emotions involved in these situations, which is one good indicator that it is a perfectly acceptable time to unleash your jokes. No one is arguing, you are not in the middle of an important emotional conversation, and you are not in a place such as someone's funeral where excessive humor would be completely inappropriate. Because you are in the right place, you can make almost any joke you want. Here are some examples of places that you can be as funny as you wish:

- Parties and casual social gatherings
- Comedy clubs
- In the breakroom with friends
- On the phone with someone you are close to
- During any other casual, non-serious events or gatherings

In addition to these three levels of "situations" you are likely to be involved in, there are a few other things you need to consider when it comes to determining whether the timing is right for a joke. The following will help you determine if the joke you want to make is acceptable for the situation or not.

Your Audience

First, you need to consider your audience. Who are you telling the joke to? How well do you know this person or these people? If you are telling the joke to someone you know well, there is a good chance that you can confidently gauge whether or not the joke will be well-received. However, if you are talking to an audience of people you don't know well, you need to censor your content. If you are talking to an audience you don't know well, *but* they have made it clear that they are not offended by the topic of the joke you want to share, then you are likely fine to share it. It is important, though, that you always know that the person will be able to take the joke properly. If there is any chance that you could seriously offend the person you are sharing the joke with, it is likely best that you hold back and don't share it. You never want your joke to come out as insensitive, cruel, or even hateful. If you want to share a racial stereotype joke, for example, make sure the person you are about to share it with isn't someone who may be offended or hurt by the joke you are sharing. Never crack jokes at the expense of someone else's happiness. If there is any way that your joke could hurt someone, then it is no longer a joke. Instead, it becomes a case of bullying. Even if you never intended to hurt someone, you might if you are not careful. Always be cautious about who is in your audience, how well you know them, and whether or not your joke could potentially hurt them in any way.

The Content of the Joke

Keep in mind the content of the joke when you are sharing it. Some people may not understand jokes at all. While it is perfectly fine to take risks, you might want to avoid making jokes that would completely fly over someone's head. For example, say the situation you are in calls for light humor, and you want to make a joke about a movie you've seen. If the person you are joking with has never seen that movie, there is a good chance they will not get the reference at all. Because you are in a situation where extensive humor isn't allowed, it may not be acceptable for you to then elaborate on the meaning of the joke and why it is funny in the first place. Instead of being funny, you might make the situation uncomfortable or otherwise awkward. You can avoid this by ensuring that the content of the joke is something that your audience is likely to understand. In some situations, particularly those where you can share as many jokes as you want, making jokes other's wouldn't understand is likely to be completely fine. You may have to explain yourself, but it should not make the situation extremely awkward or uncomfortable.

Your Environment

Always be mindful of where you are when you are making jokes, not just who you are with. If you want to make a joke that may be risqué, it is important that you are in an environment where someone will not potentially overhear your joke and become offended. Remember, just because they are not the person you are talking directly to does not mean that they are not a part of your audience if they can hear you. For example, let's say you're at a funeral for someone you hardly knew with a close friend of yours. Your friend also hardly knew the person whose funeral you are at. You may come across a joke you want to share, but based on where you are it may not be acceptable to share it. Instead of letting the joke out when you are in a room filled with grieving people who wouldn't understand, you may have more success if you say it discreetly. Such as, if you wait until you are alone elsewhere and you share the joke. You want to ensure that you are not offending anyone in your environment or otherwise being insensitive to the people in your surroundings when you are sharing a joke as this can be just as harsh as sharing an offensive joke directly with an audience of people. Remember, you never want to be hurtful towards others in your humor.

Chapter 6: Don't Be Offended

If you are going to develop a sense of humor, also take the time to learn how to stop being offended by jokes you hear. You may not be a person who tends to be offended by much, and if that is the case, then you are already well on your way. However, if you are the kind of person who tends to be offended by a large number of things, you will want to learn to let go of that. Just because your humor is not something that would offend you doesn't mean that it won't be met with humor that you may find offensive. Learning to be less offended by things means that you can stop taking situations so seriously and enjoy the humor in them.

Even though you want to reduce your tendency of being offended overall, this does not mean that you cannot still feel sensitive towards certain subjects. After all, you are entitled to your own thoughts, opinions, and perception on reality. Therefore, if someone says something offensive around you or toward you, you are not expected to not feel any level of offense towards said comment or joke. The key is in your reaction, or response, to the joke. Let's look at this in greater detail, starting with why you should not be so offended when it comes to humor.

Why You Should Not Be Offended

Being offended by someone's jokes can be frustrating, especially if you are all simply trying to enjoy yourselves. However, just because you are offended does not necessarily mean you need to express yourself about your offense. When you find that you are the kind of person who is easily offended by things, you make it difficult for people to be comfortable around you. When you share your sense of humor with them, they may be scared to share theirs with you in case you turn their joke into something serious. This can make situations uncomfortable, and can even lead to you having a reduced sense of humor since everyone around you seems to be so serious all the time.

Spending too much time being offended by things can be frustrating and downright stressful. It can damage your relationships with people and stop them from ever relaxing around you for fear of hurting your feelings. Instead of spending time with you, they will spend time with someone else who is less likely to make them feel bad for having their own sense of humor.

Another reason you want to avoid being offended all of the time is that many of the best jokes have some form of offensive undertone. For example, we have referred to the category of stereotypical racial jokes a few times in this book. These jokes are often extremely funny, especially when everyone takes the time to realize they are a joke. However, some people may choose to take offense to them, and therefore the joke becomes hurtful or hateful. The offense often takes the joke completely out of context, typically going overboard on the underlying meaning. In many circumstances, the joke-teller was simply using an opportunity to be funny. By turning it into something hateful or mean, the listener then makes it seem as though the person was intentionally being rude. This ruins the entire mood and turns an innocent joke into a problem when a problem should have never started. Now, naturally, there are some jokes that are going to be offensive. For example, a racial stereotypical joke that had something mean to it. Calling someone a derogatory name and calling it a joke, for example, would not be funny. That is bullying that is attempting to be disguised as humor. This is a completely different topic that goes beyond the realms of humor, so naturally, they do not apply to the "don't be offended" rule.

How to Stop Being Offended

It may seem straightforward, but the best way to stop being offended is to choose that you do not want to be offended by jokes. When people are joking, they are generally just trying to be funny. Many jokes touch down on sensitive subjects, especially since humor is a common coping mechanism for difficult situations and topics for many people. Recognizing that people are genuinely trying to be funny, or that they may be extremely uncomfortable in the situation, is a great way to reframe it so that you do not feel the need to be offended.

By choosing not to be offended, you choose that you are not willing to let the subject of a mere joke hurt your feelings. Again, this does not apply to bullying that is being disguised as a joke. This is pertaining to true jokes that are simply meant to be funny. You do not want to be the person who takes humor and turns it into something harsh and mean. Instead, be the person who knows how to take a joke and is willing to laugh or at least appreciate a good joke. That way, people will be more likely to appreciate and accept your humor in return.

Another thing you should pay attention to is this: someone else's joke is not a direct attack on you. Therefore, you do not have to treat it like a direct attack on you. You have every right to see a joke for what it is and not let it get personal. By choosing to see a joke for what it is, you eliminate the potentially hurtful element that you add to the situation when you choose to be offended. True jokes are not meant to be hurtful or hateful jabs at someone else. They are simply jokes that are intended to shed light on any given situation.

When You Should Verbalize the Offense

As we have been touching on, there are certain times when being offended is completely warranted. Perhaps the joke is something that is meant to you or was intended to be hurtful. If this is the case, it is completely acceptable to verbalize your offense and ask the joke-teller to be more sensitive on this subject when they are talking to you. If they are making a racial or cultural joke that you find hurtful, for example, don't be afraid to verbalize this. Or, perhaps they are making fun of a certain physical feature you have that you are sensitive about. Don't be afraid to tell them it is an out-of-bounds subject and that they should not joke about that topic with you. If you feel that they are not respecting your boundaries, never be afraid to take necessary action to end the situation. Leave, tell your boss, or if you feel it is warranted, you can even call the authorities. Protecting your rights is never wrong.

Chapter 7: Master Your Signature Joke

Every comedian has a signature joke! If you want to be funny, you need to have one, too. This joke gives you the opportunity to have a "fall back" joke to break the ice, something to share when you are getting to know someone or even something to tell at holiday parties when everyone is in the spirit for laughter. A good signature joke is a powerful asset, especially when you are learning to be funny. Learning to master this joke not only gives you something to share with others, but it also gives you something to practice all of your joke-telling skills on. Let's take a look at how you can create and master your signature joke!

Choose Something Genuinely Funny

Since your signature joke is a joke, after all, it is important that you pick something that is genuinely funny. Many people make their signature joke something that is lackluster and not interesting. Because of their failure to make this important step successful, they find themselves having very little response to their joke. They end up being the person at the holiday party telling their lame joke *yet again* by the punch bowl. Don't be that person.

Choose a joke that is actually likely to make people laugh. Find a way to bring humor into something that has happened to you in your life, or to take a generic joke and put a unique twist on it. Your joke may be a one-liner, or it may be a story you tell that makes people laugh every time. Whatever it is, make sure it is something that people can genuinely laugh at, not laugh out of pity.

Pick Something You Know Well

When you are making a joke your signature joke, you want to pick something you know well. This should be a subject or memory that you know clearly. Knowing the subject well means that you are likely to have a strong emotional attachment to it in some way or another. Either you are passionate about the subject, or you personally laugh every time you recall the memory. Having some form of emotional attachment to the joke itself makes it significantly easier for you to infuse it with emotion. Because there is already some form of emotional attachment, you can easily spice it up and exaggerate the emotion to make it even funnier.

The other important part of knowing the subject well is that it prevents you from telling a joke that you don't fully understand. For example, if you are completely clueless when it comes to computer programming but you are attempting to tell a joke about computer programming that requires intellect and a certain degree of understanding, there is a good chance that your joke will have holes in it. Either it will not make sense or it will address various elements inaccurately, making your joke sound uneducated rather than funny. While this may be a part of the joke itself, it can also lead to an awkward situation. Instead, try picking something you know well that is easy for you to talk about.

Practice It on People You Know

Start by practicing your signature joke on people you already know. Remember, your friends, family, and close co-workers are more likely to be forgiving if the joke doesn't turn out so well the first few times around. Not only will this help you get to know your joke on a more intimate level, but it will also help you grow more confident in telling your joke. Essentially, practicing means that you can easily get used to how you want to word your joke, how it sounds out loud, and the tone of voice you want to use.

When you are practicing, refrain from practicing on the same people over and over. If they have already heard the joke, they are less likely to have a positive or humorous response to it the second time around. This means that even if the second time you tell it you do much better, they will likely not laugh as much as someone else might because they already knew what to expect. Test it out on different people who are close to you so that their reaction is authentic and honest.

Adjust Your Joke

As you practice telling your joke, make sure you spend some time adjusting it. Look for ways that you can make the joke funnier, or that you can get a better reaction out of people. Maybe you can time it differently, share the punchline at a different time, or even change the emotion behind the joke itself so that your tone of voice is different. Play around with it and look to see what way you can maximize the reaction you get from your joke. You may even decide that you like telling the joke in a couple of ways, so you tell it differently depending on who you are sharing it with and what the circumstances are.

Adjusting your joke during the practice phase ensures that you are well-versed when it comes to using it out in public. For example, if you have adjusted it and perfected it with your friends and family, the first time you use it at work it is likely to be a great success rather than a joke you stumble over. Adjust it enough that it works, and that you build your confidence in telling it.

Refine Your Talent

In addition to adjusting your joke, you need to refine your talent.
The joke may be powerful, but if you are no good at telling it, then
you may have a problem on your hands. Practice how you express
emotion in your own voice. Look for opportunities elsewhere in
life, such as in regular conversation, where you can practice using
different forms of emotion in your voice. As well, you can practice
your body language. Practicing these types of things elsewhere in
life, outside of your joke, is a great way to make them come more
naturally to you. When they do, you will have greater success when
you are using these skills with your joke.

Using these skills with your joke isn't the only way you will benefit
from them, either. In fact, the more you practice these skills, in
general, the easier it will be for you to make any joke. Because you
will naturally know how to use your body language and tone of
voice to make a joke work, it will be much easier for you to nail it
the first time than it would be if you didn't practice these skills.

Let the Joke Naturally Evolve

Over time, your joke is going to evolve naturally. This will be the
result of you adjusting it and refining your skills. Let this happen,
as this will not only help your joke get better but it will also help in

keeping it as your signature joke. Come at it from different angles, tell it in different ways, and look for the opportunity to pull different punchlines out of your joke. When you do this, you allow your sense of humor to evolve alongside your joke naturally, which is also important.

Develop a Handful of Signature Jokes

Another step you can use to avoid becoming the person by the punch bowl with the same joke to tell as last year is to develop a handful of signature jokes! If you find yourself pulling on this joke often, it may be time to switch it up. Once you have perfected your initial signature joke, create a few more. Practice them, refine them, and use them whenever the situation warrants it. Having a handful of jokes will stop you from becoming boring or predictable. It also prevents you from getting too comfortable with one specific sense of humor and therefore not expanding on it. If you get too comfortable with one single joke, you may find that you still struggle with others. Let yourself branch out, step outside of your comfort zone, and keep things fresh and interesting by having a few different signature jokes.

Chapter 8: Have a Little Edge

Don't be afraid to have some edge in your comedy! Some of the best comedians touch on sensitive societal subjects in a humorous way. Many people find this to be funny since often these topics are very heavy and carry many conflicting and painful emotions. By being able to laugh at them, they not only shed light on important subjects but also help make them easier to talk about. Finally, whether we like it or not, people also tend to find this stuff hilarious.

Having an edge in your sense of humor is a great way to increase your skills and have greater success with your talent. Find opportunities to come at things from a unique angle, don't be afraid to use risqué jokes, and if you're comfortable enough, joke about things that generally make people uncomfortable. It is not a bad thing to be able to laugh at these subjects.

One reason many people don't want to have a little edge in their humor is that they are afraid to show a darker side of themselves. We are often taught to show ourselves in a positive light, so intentionally shining alight on our darker sides can be nerve-wracking. You might fear what people will think of you or what they might say in response to your joke. Remember back to chapter 1 where we discussed not being afraid to take risks. Not everyone is going to appreciate your sense of humor, and that is okay. However, as long as you appreciate your sense of humor and you are not intentionally or directly hurting anyone, there is no problem with you having a darker side to your comedy. As we have already mentioned, most famous comedians have this darker side, and it is often the part that people are drawn to the most.

Most artists, including entertainers such as those who are interested in comedy, have many positive personality traits to them. They also tend to be hostile and impulsive according to many studies done by psychologists. These last two traits are something almost everyone experiences, but many don't like to talk about. They are often frowned upon and considered "bad" in our society. However, that doesn't mean you shouldn't talk about them. Shining a light on your own hostile and impulsive thoughts and tendencies is a great way to make yourself relatable and to take the pressure off of a situation. When people realize they don't have to censor these natural parts of themselves, they are much more likely to relax around you and enjoy your sense of humor.

So, don't be afraid to be edgy. Take risks, dare to share the risqué jokes, and don't censor the part of yourself that we all secretly have inside of us. You are not likely to be viewed as horrible, mean, or otherwise bad. Unless, of course, your timing is off. However, in most scenarios as long as you use the right timing and pay attention to other important elements of the environment and your audience, these jokes should be well-received.

Chapter 9: Maximize Your Success with These Steps

You have turned to this book as an opportunity to learn how you can be funnier. You want to have a better sense of humor, you want to learn how to take things more lightly, and you want to be more playful in your life. That is why you are looking to increase your ability to successfully use comedy and conversational humor.

After reading the last seven chapters, you have been introduced to the seven most important steps that you need to know to develop a great sense of humor and become funnier to others. Although each step was explained in detail, you may be wondering how you can derive greater value from this book. After all, many of these steps are easy to do, but there also happens to be many steps. Seven may seem small in the grand scheme of things, but trying to remember all of these different tips and points each time you find yourself in a position where humor can be applied will likely kill the mood. Because you will be so invested in the details and trying to remember what's what, you will likely struggle to actually get the joke out effectively. For that reason, we have included this extra chapter to help you with the implementation process!

First, it is important that you start small. Don't try and master all seven steps in one go. If you do, you are simply going to get overwhelmed and struggle to effectively take advantage of situations where you are given the opportunity to be funny! Instead, pay attention to this book one chapter at a time. Follow the steps in order and take your time developing them. Use every opportunity you get to practice them and don't move forward until you have mastered each unique step. Once you have mastered one, layer another on top. Doing it slowly like this will ensure that you build your sense of humor on a solid foundation and that you are not left trying to put all of the pieces together with nothing to lay them on.

Another thing you need to pay attention to is this: *stop worrying about what other people think.* Yes, there are certain situations where you absolutely should not use certain jokes. You do not want to be considered insensitive, rude, offensive, or even hateful for a joke you make. Using the wrong timing, speaking to the wrong audience, or wording yourself wrong can all contribute to your sense of humor being thrown out the window and the situation going horribly wrong. Other than these obvious situations, however, do not be afraid of what other people think. If you have an incredibly dry and juvenile sense of humor, own it. If you are into risqué jokes, own it. If you like to tell jokes in the form of stories or make fun of your own life, go for it. Never worry about what other people think of your jokes. Your sense of humor is unique to you, and it should not concern anyone else. Give yourself the benefit of the doubt, allow yourself to let go of it when people don't like you and own the jokes you share. Comedians don't abandon their sense of humor for a few disapproving people, and neither should you.

Conclusion

Thanks again for reading *"How to Be Funny: The Right Way"*!

This book was designed to help you increase your sense of humor and learn to be funnier! Whether you want to master comedy itself, get better with conversational humor, or simply make people laugh more, this book was created to help you out.

I hope you were able to learn plenty about the art of comedy through this book. Through the simple-to-follow seven-step process, you were given the only seven steps you need to be a funnier person overall. Not only will these tips help you become funnier to yourself, but they will also help your humor be better delivered and therefore more well-received. I hope that by following each step and mastering them all, you can have better luck making people laugh and lightening up the mood. There is great value in adding a sense of playfulness to your life, which you learn as you become a funnier person.

The next step is to practice being funny! Follow the steps in order and master them one at a time. Practice at every chance you have, whether it's with family and friends, coworkers, or even a stranger at the gas station. You never have to work too hard to find someone who is willing to listen to you crack jokes. Most people are looking to smile more, so as long as you are willing to be that person, they will listen!

Remember to pay attention to important things such as who your audience is, where you are, the timing, and what the content of your joke is. Ensuring that you keep these aspects properly monitored will prevent you from accidentally hurting someone's feelings or turning an otherwise serious situation into something awkward. You don't want people to think you are insensitive or rude because you don't know how to pick the right place and time to have a sense of humor! If everything aligns just right, though, don't be afraid to take risks! Say things people are thinking but are afraid to admit themselves, and don't be scared to honor your personal comedic style. You will be grateful that you did, and so will the people rolling with laughter as a result of your jokes.

Thank you, and enjoy cracking jokes and being funny to your friends! Continue to making other people laugh and happy!

More by Dean Mack

Discover all books from the Social Skills Best Seller Series by Dean Mack at:

bit.ly/dean-mack

Book 1: *How to Flirt*

Book 2: *How to Start a Conversation*

Book 3: *How to Talk to People*

Book 4: *How to Ask Questions*

Book 5: *How to Be Funny*

Book 6: *How to Influence People*

Book 7: *How to Attract Men*

Book 8: *How to Attract Women*

Themed book bundles available at discounted prices:

bit.ly/dean-mack